Dining Room Dispatches

A YEAR OF CURATED MUSINGS ON LIFE AND HOME

Amy Mangan

FOREWORD BY FRANCES SCHULTZ

BLACK ROSE WRITING | TEXAS

© 2022 by Amy Mangan
All rights reserved. No part of this book may be reproduced, stored in a retrieval system or transmitted in any form or by any means without the prior written permission of the publishers, except by a reviewer who may quote brief passages in a review to be printed in a newspaper, magazine or journal.

The author grants the final approval of this literary material.

First printing / First Hardcover printing

ISBN: 978-1-68513-098-5 (Paperback); 978-1-68513-099-2 (Hardcover)
PUBLISHED BY BLACK ROSE WRITING
www.blackrosewriting.com

Printed in the United States of America
Suggested retail price (SRP): $24.95 (Paperback); $29.95 (Hardcover)

Dining Room Dispatches is printed in Benton Modern

Cover images by Kristie Griggs.
Photographs by Kristie Griggs, John Jernigan, and Dave Miller; or provided.
Painting of home on title page by Micah Lomel.
Book design by Steven J. Codraro.

*As a planet-friendly publisher, Black Rose Writing does its best to eliminate unnecessary waste to reduce paper usage and energy costs, while never compromising the reading experience. As a result, the final word count vs. page count may not meet common expectations.

Also by Amy Mangan

This Side Up:
The Road to
a Renovated Life
A MEMOIR

ACCENT PIECES:
Collected Writings and
Moments that Decorate
Our Lives

**The History
Lesson**
A NOVEL

ESSAYS AND COLUMNS

Salon	Southern Living	Ocala Magazine
Better Homes and Gardens	Southern Accents	Ocala Star Banner
	Thrive Global	Ocala Style

To my husband and children

Each day is a good one because of you

Contents

Foreword...xi

Introduction...xiii

January

CENTERPIECES: Plan 3 | Not the Home of My Dreams 4 | To All the Diet Books I've Loved Before 7 | Road to Parnassus 9 | Patterns 10 | On the Nature of Mike 13 | Virtual Reality 15 | Vision Quest 16 | The Table 19 | An Old-Fashioned Life 20 | Being Mama 22 | Patina 23

February

CENTERPIECES: Inspire 26 | A Steaming Cup of Perspective 29 | Soup for Placemats 30 | Bamboo Beauty 32 | A Moment with Carolanne Roberts 34 | Two Dog Night 41 | I Must Dance 42 | Hot Time in the Studio 44 | Favorite Find: Wall of Love 45 | Poppyseed Ministry 46 | Camellia 48

March

CENTERPIECES: Listen 53 | The Girl Wore Prada 54 | A Moment with Cass Roth Retz 56 | Watch List: All Creatures Great and Small 59 | Obituary 60 | 'Nati Nights 62 | What's In a Name 64

April

CENTERPIECES: Grace 68 | Some Bunny Loves You 70 | Food Coordinator 72 | Bedside Notes 74 | Gimlets and Checklists 76 | A Moment with Erin Sparks 78 | Spoiling With Love 83 | Slow Down, Honey 85

May

CENTERPIECES: Adjust 89 | What May Come and Go, Some Things Will Remain 90 | Of Mandolins and Memories 92 | Signs of Leaf 95 | The Unexpected Gift of Passion 96 | A Moment with Jose Juarez 98 | Savoring Shermans on Doris Drive 102 | Living Room 105 | The Chair 106

June

CENTERPIECES: Revel 110 | Little Miss Something 112 | The Kitchen 114 | Scar of Florida 116 | A Treasure with Genuine Class 118 | Café Lights 120 | Powerball Dreaming 122 | A Moment with Karley Holland 124 | Meeting a Legend 128

July

CENTERPIECES: Protect **134** | The Reading Worm **136** | I ♥ My Friends **138** | Serenading the Summer of Mary Kay **140** | Amid Any Storm, Try Not to Be a Label Maker **142** | A Word from a Digitized Elder **144** | The Rhinestone Writer **146**

August

CENTERPIECES: Reflect **150** | Booking a Dream **152** | Go-To Friends **154** | Dad's Crowning Glory **156** | Field of Screams **158** | A Moment with Grace Hamlin **160** | The Road of What Ifs: A Birthday Reflection **164** | Facebook's Four Stages of "This Can't Be" **166**

September

CENTERPIECES: Pace **170** | Looking at the Bright Side **172** | Faux Real **175** | Living Your Personal Yes **176** | Meaning of Correspondence **178** | Flannel Fashionista **180** | Slow Going Toward the Glass Menagerie **182**

October

CENTERPIECES: Indulge **186** | Hay Bales of Gratitude **188** | Sometimes the Biggest Thrill is Standing Tall **190** | Listless and Love it **192** | A Moment with Ashton McLeod **194** | Listening Party **198**

November

CENTERPIECES: Embrace **202** | Someone Left the Cake Out in the Rain **204** | Old but New **207** | A Moment with Crystal Flynn **208** | Why I Believe in Phone-Loving Millennials **212** | Friendsgiving **216** | Thankful **218**

December

CENTERPIECES: Celebrate **222** | Mama's Pistachio Cake **224** | Sticks of Love **226** | Nancy With the Smiling Place **229** | Best Wedding Christmas Tree Ever **230** | Good Lasso Tidings to You **232** | Two of a Kind **235**

Acknowledgments

Author, artist, life coach, entertainer and tastemaker extraordinaire, Frances Schultz understands the virtue of embracing and chronicling life. Her talents can be found on her website *francesschultz.com* and *@francesschultz* on Instagram. Her books include *California Cooking and Southern Style* and *The Bee Cottage Story*.

Foreword
by Frances Schultz

What a jewel is Amy Mangan and what pearls are her *Dining Room Dispatches*. I say pearls because they are lustrous, reflective, and complete in themselves, each beautiful alone and also stunning when strung together. Like pearls, they are also imminently wearable, figuratively speaking, with our everyday selves in our everyday lives, appropriate and elegant. As pearls enhance the beauty of the wearer (flattering to all faces!), so do Amy's roving and thoughtful reflections, each culminating in a loving prompt to take a specific action to embrace and enrich your own life.

As a lifelong writer of books and articles about houses and how our homes reflect our lives, I deeply appreciate Amy's instinctive understanding of how our living spaces reflect our lives, and vice versa.

I've had the privilege of knowing and working with Amy for nearly two years, and I am continuously impressed, inspired, and touched by her honesty, her insight, her courage, her vulnerability, her magnanimity, and her gentle humor—all of which come through in her writing. You will be too.

You don't need to know Amy long to get why people call her "Mama Mangz," and I mean lots of people, from her children's friends, to her readers and fans, and community. This charming and wise book of *Dining Room Dispatches* gives us one more reason to love Mama Mangz.

Introduction

I own three dining room tables. Most of this book has been written on one of them. My home is small with one main living area nestled in between bedrooms, baths, pantry, and the kitchen. My friend Kelly calls it a "jewel box", a title which suits the one-story home just fine. Except there's not a lot of room for jewelry or, in this case, tables. And, yet.

The first table that came into my life arrived as my marriage to Mike began. His late great aunt's mahogany dining table is something I imagined would go nicely on a Downton Abbey set. With pull-out leaves on either end, it seats eight, but today, seats one. We use it for Mike's home office desk. The next table belonged to a dear friend who was downsizing, so I upsized her cottage-style, distressed cream-painted piece of furniture that sits by a corner window in the living room. Nearby is the newest addition to the furniture family, an oblong Oak claw foot table, that is, lo and behold, used for dining. And, if we're being picky, I have four tables if I count Mama's cherry-twist side piece in the kitchen. Wait. Make that five. I just purchased a white bamboo round dining table for my new home office which I've claimed in the spare bedroom so Mike and I can live in harmony with our own work spaces.

Clearly, I have a table problem. Or do I?

So much has happened around these beloved acquisitions — family dinners, holiday meals, birthdays, anniversaries, homework, happy hours, puzzle nights, game nights, you-name-it nights, and — my favorite of all — conversations between friends and family who feel compelled to stay a while and visit just a little longer. Elbows on table, wine in hand, heart to heart.

Which led me to this book. These monthly passages are my way of honoring the beautiful nuances of the way we spend our lives. The way we wake up, work, play, hope and dream. It's my tribute to the right now and the right around the corner. To the goodness of a day well spent and times we're ready to close the curtains ready for a new morning. I've also added a "Set Your Table" call to action inviting you to participate in something that restores and rejuvenates. Once a month, you'll see an entry dedicated to "Centerpieces" – one seminal word that captures an intention.

You may choose to read in sequence or skip around depending on the season of your life. Whatever you do, I wish you for you a glorious year of gathering within and beyond, elbow to elbow, heart to heart.

Amy

January

Centerpieces: Plan

I appreciate consistency especially when it comes to money. A steady paycheck solves a lot of life's ills. I realize that quality of life encompasses more than one's bank account, but so does peace of mind and I've experienced a scarcity of both. It ain't fun.

To me, this type of abundance equals certainty—enough for the necessary like food, shelter, retirement, longterm care, inheritance for our kids and just enough for meaningful experiences like travel, concerts, and, of course, decorating. Mike informed me the latter could not be considered a necessity.

We're approaching this goal with what I've termed our "Peace of Mind Plan." Sure, we've crafted a crateful of budgets throughout the years. This strategy is different because we began with listing what would give us peace of mind, then developed a way to get there. This may put a dent in my HomeGoods spending which a friend of mine's husband calls "the place you go to buy stuff you don't need." And that's okay.

SET YOUR TABLE

What gives you peace of mind? Commit to a way to reach emotional nirvana.

Not the Home of My Dreams

It's that time of year again and I'm resisting the temptation to continue an annual tradition. I'm not talking about making New Year's resolutions, most of which I won't keep (I'm looking at you, Weight Watchers.)

Every January, the network debuts its latest Dream Home Giveaway. Mountains, beaches, bucolic vineyards, and apple orchards—you name the picturesque location, they've built it. And you, dear friend, can be a winner! The house, the new Jeep Grand Wagoneer and a lotta cash from Rocket Mortgage (product placement, anyone?) Go on, give it a try. I wish you Godspeed. I'm out.

For years, I've entered the contest by submitting an online entry—twice daily!—both on HGTV and Food Network. To give me an extra advantage, I signed up for every newsletter and blog. Now I average 200 daily emails. I "like" every HGTV social media post. Surely, they're noticing me, right?

And when that magical day arrives with a two-hour television spectacular reveal of the winner, I'm not one of them. I'm at home. As in, *not* with the top three contenders shown on the television screen. By the house. The one I won't win.

I look around. I'm in my neutral-bathed living room, a serene space that lowers my blood pressure the minute I walk in. I'm sitting in one of the armchairs upholstered in cream and teal leopard fabric that matches the pillows on the slipper chairs, all found at estate sales. My husband, Mike, is by me. I'm surrounded by love. I've worked hard to get to this place, literally, financially, emotionally. It's my sacred nest, a small one-story New Orleans-style structure that is home. Each room, each accent piece, the creaky back door, café lights outside, every framed photo of family and friends. And it's enough. More than enough, really.

I once dreamed of a grand residence overflowing with square footage and custom crown molding. That's just a house. It's good to be in the home of *my* dreams.

SET YOUR TABLE

Find your favorite place—wherever you define as home. Write down what that means to you.

To All the Diet Books I've Loved Before

Maybe this month should be called "Things I Quit." My past list was long, chock full of gym memberships, TV streaming services, phone apps, swearing off sweets (failed), vodka (yeah, right), magazine subscriptions, Amazon, and Diet Cokes with crushed ice from my beloved Hungry Bear Drive-In (c'mon, it's good for the economy). This year, I've modified my approach to focus on habits that seem less obvious, yet, equally disruptive.

THINGS TO STOP THIS YEAR

- *Saying "lean in" because it appears in the Magna Carta of corporate speak.*
- *Saying "I'm sorry" during conversations that don't merit an apology like at work—"I'm sorry, I have a question." It's good to clarify when appropriate. Or personal—"I'm sorry, I can't make it." Simply, "I can't make it, but thank you for asking" suffices.*
- *Doing more work than humanly possible.*
- *Staying up late.*

THINGS I'M GOING TO START

- *Walk, write and pray each day. • Nourish uplifting friendships.*
- *Go to bed by 10 p.m.*
- *Create more meaningful experiences with loved ones.*

Noticeably absent is any reference to food. Maybe this is because in my adult life, I have purchased enough healthy eating and nutrition books to feed an army of very hungry dieters. I'm reading a new one, heavy on veggies, light on cheese. I'll give it try. However, this year, I won't feel guilty if I add it to the pile of misfit health books right next to the dusty weights, jump rope and yoga mat. Sorry, not sorry.

=== **SET YOUR TABLE** ===

*What have you quit? Good for you.
Now think about what is worth starting.*

Road to Parnassus

Many destinations remain on my travel bucket list. France. Ireland. 3900 Hillsboro Pike #14 in Nashville. Don't tell me you've been there. I'll corner you for the next hour to share every single detail. Parnassus Books, the said destination address, is the literary genius creation of a bookstore owned by Ann Patchett, an actual literary genius.

I remember the first time I read Patchett like I remember the first time I met Mike. Both were beautifully memorable. The Patchett meet-cute: I was a mom to an eight and 10-year-old, full-time college professor and writer struggling to put two words together at 10 pm after the kids went to bed and my class papers were graded. Clearly, I needed a diversion. Escaping to the local bookstore, I thumbed through new nonfiction, my go-to. *Truth & Beauty* caught my eye—Patchett's moving tribute to friendship with the late writer Lucy Grealy. I read it in two days, breaking only to attend to necessities like working and eating. And helping the kids with homework. I was hooked.

Since that time, a lot has changed for Ann and me (subtle switch to first name use like we're buddies.) She's written more award-winning books and opened a bookstore to support authors and reading. I'm. Not. Worthy. Independent bookstores have suffered mightily at the hand of Amazon and the pandemic, yet, Parnassus Books has thrived. I'd like to think Ann's vision and reputation is a large reason why.

I have never felt as home as I do in a bookstore. "Getting lost in a bookstore" is our family's favorite saying and activity. Which is why I want to go to Parnassus. Ann may not be there and that's okay. Her presence will be. And endless shelves of words waiting to be read.

SET YOUR TABLE

Name one adventure you want to experience this year. Jot it on a notecard and put it somewhere you see every single day until you do it.

Patterns

Lifelong friend Kelly says her most telling high school memory of me was sitting in my bedroom on a Friday night hanging ceramic tiles on my wall while listening to Amy Grant. Stunning to think I didn't make homecoming court.

The tiles came from one of Dad's construction sites. As a residential builder, he brought home project leftovers—scraps of wood, flooring, sheetrock, wallpaper, lights, doors, even fireplace mantels. His workshop was a stand-alone structure next to our garage and it was Christmas every day for his design-loving youngest daughter. One day, I spotted four large rectangular tiles painted light blue with a delicate white flower. Grabbing the tiles, I rushed inside scheming for the perfect spot to hang them. Days, then weeks, went by as the ceramic pieces lay on my bedroom floor. I kept rearranging them—two on top, two on bottom then all lined up in a single row, then spread out to create a diamond. The possibilities were endless! So was my BFF's patience.

"Wanna go to the mall?" Kelly would ask for the umpteenth time.

Why go out when we can shop at Dad's garage? Lucky for me, Kelly was very patient. Kneeling down beside me, she moved the tiles around in a pattern that turned out to be exactly what I was hoping for. They stayed in that very formation on my bedroom wall until I moved out after college.

It's funny how much happiness those darn tiles gave me. And the subsequent joy that picture frames, art and light sconces continue to provide. My current vibe is MixTiles, removable framed pics from my cell phone camera, though I'm running out of walls. I've found comfort in the regularity of arranging things, each space offering a new chance to create something that marries order and beauty. And when a spot feels stale, I simply move a few things around until it feels right.

I've done this in my life, too, shifting and rearranging. Sometimes my life design has gone off kilter, but a tweak here and shift there usually ends up better than the original plan. As a teenager, I played Amy Grant's song "Brand New Start" over and over. I found comfort in knowing each day brought new beginnings. And maybe also something beautiful waiting for me to find it the perfect spot.

SET YOUR TABLE

Today, look at the patterns in your life.
Find one piece of furniture that fills your heart.

On the Nature of Mike

Coltrane, Baker, Evans. All three came into my relationship with Mike, blessed be. Before him, my playlist was comprised of great classics like Super Freak. This is his birthday month. Over the years, I've refined just exactly what this celebration means. It's all the big milestones and the satisfying in-betweens, subtle nuances of connections that bridge the organic with memorable. Like long walks together in our historic neighborhood. Going to classics and cocktails movie nights at the downtown theater. Reading the newspaper side by side. And, always, listening to music.

Mike recently shared a new favorite—Max Richter, a contemporary musician who's composed breathtaking soundtracks and bravely tackled a new take on Vivaldi's "Four Seasons." Now I have on repeat Richter's "On the Nature of Daylight," a signature piece for film and television, namely the movie "Arrival." Slow and cyclical with an intertwined string ensemble, the song reaches a moving crescendo with a subtle fierceness that, inevitably, takes me to undiscovered emotional territory.

Kind of like Mike, blessed be.

SET YOUR TABLE

Play Max Richter's "On the Nature of Daylight" and "Mercy." I bet you'll have all the feels.

On the Nature of Daylight

Mercy

Virtual Reality

One silver lining of this awful pandemic has been found in creating new and surprising connections with other humans. While we are all pretty worn out staring in front of computer screens, I've discovered the virtue in virtual.

As an empty nester, I miss my young adult children, neither of whom live close by. And I miss extended family and dear friends. I once could hop on a plane or take a road trip to visit them without checking my temperature. Now, I'm turning on the computer to say hi. Here's a few ways that have helped:

Virtual Family Night: Even though we talk throughout the month, we dedicate one night for a topical conversation via Zoom or Facetime. We'll focus our discussion about a movie, book, article or political issue du jour and rotate who chooses for the month. Compliments of Mom and Dad, we each order delivery and munch and chat till our hearts, minds and stomachs are content.

Virtual Movie/Travel/Reading/You Name It Club: If you know me or have read my previous work, you know I love me some Movie Club, my 20-year group of friends who love films and each other. Not only do we still try to gather for regular movie nights, albeit via a computer screen to discuss post-viewing, but we've also become the travel club, taking one trip a year—these days in between COVID variants. We're also the reading club, sharing favorite books and, inevitably, talking about them.

Virtual Cocktail Hour: Who hasn't done this? It's so easy and fun and there's vodka! I belong to a monthly happy hour with friends who are scattered everywhere so it's a mini reunion. We also have a group text that is an automatic mood booster.

With or without a universal health crisis, I hope these new engagements stick around for a very long time.

SET YOUR TABLE

Commit to one virtual experience with someone. Cocktail optional, but I highly recommend it.

Vision Quest

The new year always invites a time of reflection and, usually, a handful of aspirational goals. I confess I'm one of those who annually creates a vision board complete with dreams written in colorful Sharpies and glued-on magazine images. I'm pretty good at maintaining focus until life and personal discipline starts to unravel by April. Last year, however, I implemented a new stick-to-it-ness approach I call "The Mangan Stick-to-It-ness Approach." MasterClass should be calling any day now.

First, I answered the question: What do I want from my life? For me, it came down to four intentions: Meaningful experiences and relationships with loved ones, work that connects and inspires, good health, and financial security. I didn't try to arrive at a certain number, but four felt right.

Next, I transferred above goals to my vision board. Then, I placed the 8 x 10 board on an easel on my home office desk where I see it every day. Each morning I take these goals into a practice I started last year, waking 30 minutes early to write my four intentions into my journal with actions I can do that day. Not the next day. Or the next month. *That* day. If I miss a day, I feel it in my bones. Maybe it was this approach, maybe it was being home more, but I realized a lot of my intentions.

Here's the thing: it's not the grand sweeping dream of a lifetime that is attainable. Rather, for me at least, it's the tiny micro steps in a lovely, single 24 hours that brings a sense of wholeness. I don't always get it right, but I get it done.

How often I told my children when they were young and struggling with something that "done is better than perfect." Who really remembers anyone's fifth grade science project? This isn't the same as accepting mediocrity. It's accepting what's worth the full-scale investment of energy versus it'll do effort.

As I write, I see my current vision board with the cut-out clippings of the ocean and the Eiffel Tower beside the bold words "joy" and "transformation." And individual parent/child trips! I see someone—ahem, me—cut out of an image from my last book, *Accent Pieces*.

Go for it, Girl. What a vision.

SET YOUR TABLE

You don't need art supplies to create your vision. A notepad will do. Just do this: Write it down. Make a copy and send to a friend you can trust will follow up with you on a regular basis.

The Table

It's been established I have an abundance of dining room tables. The last one wasn't my fault. I couldn't help it that the existing whitewashed table, given to me by a very dear and incredibly stylish friend, was too small.

One day over holiday when my daughter Gillian was home, I mentioned it felt a bit crowded. That's when she said, "Mama, that's because it is *tooooo* small."

The search began with a very limited budget. A friend told me to look at Facebook Marketplace. Right as I clicked, a gorgeous oak claw-foot table appeared. With a leaf! It was insanely underpriced. Two clicks later, I was the owner. Two days later, the table sat beneath my white pagoda chandelier. This is what love feels like.

Even better, it reminded me of Mama and her oblong oak table that served many a Sunday lunch after church. She never minded when a few extra showed up for her mouth-watering pot roast marinated in Italian dressing, ham hock field peas, squash casserole and biscuits with apple butter. "Grab a leaf, Sherman!" she'd yell from the kitchen. A few hours later, we were still convened at the table, a little more stuffed, but satisfied by the communion of food and spirit.

Mama, I hope my table does the same.

SET YOUR TABLE

Take a walk around your home. Find one piece of furniture, art, music collection, what have you, that speaks to you. Celebrate the love you feel staring at it face to furniture.

An Old-Fashioned Life

It's been eight days into the new year and, please, Woodford Reserve, help us all. In our 31 years of marriage, Mike has become the consummate bartender. It's not about the drink. Well, kind of. When the sun sets and I hear the cocktail shaker clink clink clink ice against metal, I'm a very thirsty Pavlov's Dog ready for his famous Maple Old Fashioned.

It's the anticipation of what's next: A delicious drink and even more delicious magic moment with the guy who taught me the difference between store-bought simple syrup and the kind you make. Chet Baker on Spotify. Candles lit. A dash of maple syrup in the mix. I'm ready.

MIKE'S MAPLE OLD FASHIONED *Yield 1 serving (so make extra!)*

INGREDIENTS

2 oz. bourbon or rye • 3-4 dashes Angostura bitters • ½ teaspoon maple syrup • Orange peel • Ice • A cherry on top

DIRECTIONS

- Use a vegetable peeler or knife to carefully cut a 3-inch-long piece of orange peel. Run the pulp side of the peel around the rim of the cocktail of the glass, then set the peel aside for later.
- Add the bourbon, bitters, and maple syrup to the glass and briefly stir. Add the ice, then stir one more time to mix and chill.
- Give the orange peel a good twist above the glass to release its oils, then tuck it into the drink. Add the cherry and serve immediately.

=== **SET YOUR TABLE** ===

This one's easy—make an Old Fashioned for the love of Woodford! Light the candles, play quiet jazz — Chet Baker never fails — and settle into your best chair. Sip and repeat.

Being Mama

A belated Christmas gift arrived in the mail today. It was addressed to Mama. While I am blessed with two incredible children by birth, the present came from someone else—Allie and Natalie—two young adults who grace me with the unofficial title as their other mother by love. Mind you, they both have amazing mothers. I just happened to win the lotto when my children selected amazing friends who, along the way, became family.

Little did I know how wonderful these amazing humans would enrich my life. I mean, who thinks that when she sees the faint pink line on the pregnancy test? "Oh happy day! I'm going to have a child! And awesome new friends!" I don't think so.

Here's what I've discovered in the afternoon of my life as Carl Jung would say—surround yourself with a diverse blend of friendships and add a little young in the mix. You'll grow in unexpected ways with their offerings of passions and thoughts. Maybe, if you're lucky they will, too.

SET YOUR TABLE

Fold in someone young into your life. Listen and learn.

Patina

There's a chip on my bedside table. My living room ottoman bears a few puppy teeth marks. In my home, dogs are love and absolved of all sins. My dining room table has few scratches, too. If I conducted an inventory of my furniture, I'm sure I'd find a few more nicks and what-have-you on most of my worldly belongings. No matter, I love 'em all.

Such markings tell me a lot about a piece and its history. The faint Sharpie black mark on the kitchen table reminds me of marathon science project nights with the kiddos. I spot nail polish remover on the corner of a lamp, taking me back to Gilly's spa-themed birthday party when she was little.

Vintage is the word of the moment in interior design where everything old is new or new-ish again. I tend to gravitate toward what is enduring, classic and, above all, interesting. Pick up one of the candle holders from my writing desk in the living room and I'll tell you about my friend Hellen who gave them to me. The glazed crackled stoneware pair each holds a tall taper candle. Melted wax remains on the base from well-lit evenings with friends and usually a glass of Sauvignon Blanc close by. Hellen has been an important part of such nights and, more specifically, the very tender parts of my life. She exudes elegance in the way she carries herself. Our friendship is enduring and true. Dare I say vintage? Both home and heart are classics worth preserving.

SET YOUR TABLE

Who are your vintage friendships? Send them a note or text and tell them. Better yet, set a date to get together.

February

Centerpieces: Inspire

When my daughter Gilly went to graduate school in Birmingham, Alabama, I was thrilled for several reasons. One, she was embarking on a true career passion to be a healthcare administrator. Two, my forever friends Carolanne and Johnny live there. And, also, I had another reason to visit my favorite hotel to purchase the best-smelling candle in all of the world.

I first stayed at Grand Bohemian Birmingham several years ago. The minute I stepped inside the grand lobby, I was entranced by the most intoxicating scent from lit candles at the check-in counter. The blend of bergamot, lavender and tobacco had me hooked. The hotel filtered the seductive scent through the room vents. Pure. Bliss. At the conclusion of my visit, I left with a box full of their candles that—lawd have mercy—were available for purchase.

In time, I went through my candle inventory. I re-ordered. Then I went through another shipment. The cycle continued until I decided supporting my daughter's higher educational goals and funding my own essentials like food and shelter were more important than an elegant glass of wax.

Gilly graduates this spring. Although she now lives in New York City for her hospital fellowship, the Mangans plan to return to Birmingham for her graduation ceremony. We're staying at the Grand Bohemian on a trip that promises to be bittersweet. I have so many fond memories of this beautiful city that introduced me to forever friends, incredible restaurants, exquisite neighborhoods, gorgeous public gardens and one grand candle. I've got my credit card ready.

SET YOUR TABLE

I believe every home should have a signature scent. Mine is bergamot, lavender and tobacco. Discover your favorite candle today.

A Steaming Cup of Perspective

Since Gilly moved to Brooklyn, I've discovered my new favorite spot: Five Leaves Café. Each morning after Gilly left for work, I walked down a brownstone-lined street to this corner café on an intersection of aliveness—a nearby park, shops, and boutique hotels.

Five Leaves' outdoor seating made me feel like I was sitting in a Paris bistro and the customer conservations to my right and left were equally vibrant. A couple next to me ran through their day's agenda—work, life, a Manhattan dinner, babysitter plans. What was that restaurant they said they loved? Shoot, speak up, people!

The next day—same place, same café table—two women beside me exchanged dating advice and admonitions. "Swipe again, honey!" one laughed when talking about a recent online dating experience. Honestly, I wasn't snooping, they were right next to me! Plus, I'm Southern which translates to a tad nosy.

These overheard snippets of life are reminders of how we are connected in our universal quest for happiness, meaningful experiences and a really good cappuccino.

SET YOUR TABLE

Where is your favorite corner of the world? Schedule time there for a little self-care—and a really good cup of coffee.

Soup for Placemats

It was an unseasonably cool and windy wintry night in Florida, so I decide to make my "everything but the kitchen sink" garden vegetable soup. Fresh carrots, tomatoes, green beans, broccoli, kale, sauteed mushrooms with onions, and a healthy dose of garlic—complemented with a toasted loaf of French bread, topped with olive oil and fresh herbs. Without a recipe, I kept adding more veggies until the pot was filled to the brim. I texted Julee, my close friend and neighbor, to let her know that a bowl of soup, bread and red wine was headed her way.

"Great! I have something for you, too!"

Of course, she does. Here's the thing about Julee—she is one of the most thoughtful, intentional friends. She has a direct radar to my soul and Amazon cart. Her gifts and gestures are spot on, zeroing into exactly what I love.

When I dropped off my culinary goodies, Julee handed me a package of placemats. They were the *exact* placemats I had recently added "to order" from one of my favorite online stores, something of which Julee was unaware. Returning home, I was now the proud owner of four Mark & Graham sky blue gingham cork placements.

Just before my first sip of soup, I said a small prayer of gratitude for the meal in front of me and my neighbor-gift-whisperer close by.

SET YOUR TABLE

Say grace for the friend who always seems to know exactly what you need.

Bamboo Beauty

I love my vintage bamboo bed that holds court in the guest bedroom. This space has also become my sweet respite in between long workdays and writing nights.

I found the bed online and painted it in a neutral bone ivory. I like letting other pieces shine in the décor spotlight instead of the furniture. So, I added some color with the neutral bedding, a chinoiserie pillow, and abstract art. This gorgeous bed isn't needy…kind of like, yeah, I'm here. I'm beautiful. You're welcome.

SET YOUR TABLE

Recipe for a calm room: Neutral colors are a perfect foundation. Got a spot that needs a refresh? Bathe it in ivory paint and furniture. Layer with carefully chosen vivid accent pieces. Let it marinate until it's ready to be your sanctuary. Enjoy!

A MOMENT WITH
Carolanne Roberts

Carolanne Roberts has graced countless pages and lives with her words, heart and zest for life. A former longtime *Southern Living* editor, her post-magazine world continues to inspire others with a popular blog, special writing assignments for special causes and entertaining friends and family in quintessential Carolanne style.

Q: You've had a remarkable and diverse journalism career. What was the most satisfying experience and why?

Carolanne: A kaleidoscope of memories rushes to my head at the very thought of satisfying experiences—might we count big-time all the times I followed my journalist mother on assignments from childhood forward (including being in the newsroom on day of the JFK assassination). There were the fashion shows in NYC, the fascinating homespun people up West Virginia hollows, and, to the point of this book, her journalistic flirtations with clothing designers and creative forces in the home design world (among her many hats were Fashion Editor and Home Furnishings Editor which meant trips to High Point and many a peek behind those magical curtains). Those stand out with me the writer-in-training, a veritable sponge to her expertise.

So what to mention next? How about the handful of years on the "star beat" where I learned to navigate egos and drill down to the real person behind the glam, many times seated in the star's own dressing room or,

better still, his/her home—stories regularly took me to Hollywood, NYC and nearby Miami from my then-Fort Lauderdale base.

Or was it the *Southern Living* years, all 26 full-time ones and a decade more as an *Southern Living* freelancer? To jump headfirst into the South's rich, layered culture, rooting out the lingering traditions laced with their modern counterparts tuned my heart to All Things Southern—my favorite moments there were the sit-down interviews with noted or "should be noted" Southerners whose imprint will be forever felt. Especially by me.

TOP: Carolanne interviewing Efrem Zimbalist, Jr.
BOTTOM: Posing questions to Robert F. Kennedy

Q: Any special stories top the list as one of your favorites?

Carolanne: That's like asking me my favorite child. So let's do it this way, by categories. Favorite "travels with mom" story: A profile of Suzanne Daché, granddaughter of then-famous milliner Lilly Daché (a big deal then!)—this story gave me a window into fame, couture style, and the ability of someone my age to make a difference.

Favorite Hollywood Years story: Actor Efrem Zimbalist Jr (star of The FBI television show). My editor, who sent The New Kid (me) to the interview with zero notice, had not-so-gently warned "He hates stupid questions and will walk out on you in a heartbeat." So Mr. Zimbalist, staring at me intently as I explained that I knew nothing about him, took a deep pause, then an even deeper breath (during which I envisioned the end of my career), and proceeded to regale me with a wonderful series of questions "you should ask me" followed by the best of answers. He later confessed he had revealed things he'd never shared. The paper was ultra impressed with my copy; I was/am forever grateful for his kindness.

Carolanne with Goldie Hawn

There are too many Southern Living stories, thousands, to choose a single—I liked the ones that shone deserved light on people making important differences for the good of the South. One involved a rural Georgia woman who started a grassroots movement to send huge containers of good condition, age-appropriate books to schools in the English-speaking countries of Africa; my story helped her form a network which grew and grew as shipments stuffed with tales left for the faraway lands.

My post-Southern Living favorites: the tale of a delightful young woman from Siberia who dreamed of buying her parents a car to replace their cantankerous, unreliable Soviet model—she did just that after graduating from high school, college and graduate schools in Mississippi (each a different level of exchange student); her hard work and tenacity won her a high-placed job in Memphis—and the ability to buy that car. This story won a national first-place award for me—and a permanent place in my heart. I've even been toying with the idea of connecting her to an American 30-something friend who majored in Russian…they're both in Tennessee. Can a romance story be on the horizon?

Q: You continue to inspire others with unique writing projects. What are you currently working on?
Carolanne: I'm currently being given the gift of a break. Like those circus performers we used to see on TV, the ones spinning a zillion dishes in the air, all the while dancing, I usually am marching to the beat of someone else's deadline. And as I write this, I'm in between deadlines. This puts me in the unaccustomed driver's seat. With choices. Shall I write a book? Fiction or non-fiction? Autobiographical or inspired by life around me? Shall I expand the blog I send out each Tuesday (currently way over 100 weeks and counting) to see if it has "legs" out in the real world, beyond the friends and friends-of-friends who read it now? Is there something else looming (inspired by Amy, perhaps!).

I fully expect to use this blank slate, cementing a direction before the freelance requests return as they always seem to do. If you love a good mystery, I'm all that. The whodunit in the tale will be a very busy me.

Q: As a grateful guest in your homes, tell me how you create your own *Southern Living* sense of style.
Carolanne: Our style, no matter where we go, is All About Us. There's not a room in our life that isn't graced by objects, photos, keepsakes, books, travel memories, etc., that reflect our own lives. Yes, we work with our beloved Diane the Decorator on any changes, and she coaxes us (me!) into banishing unseemly items that have followed us for decades after being in the family as far back as the 1800s (in other words, "ugly sentimental" goes to the basement or trash bin). Having been owned by an ancestor isn't enough—but something great from the family is heaven-on-earth if it works in the room. Sense of place factors in too—our mountain home features framed architectural drawings of the church where we married. In frames, they are pure art and so very "us." At our lake house, sited near a certain university football stadium, you'll find some vintage/tasteful items that salute the team; a framed enlargement of Johnny's great-grandfather and the 1887 Penn State football team (its first) holds a place of honor alongside artwork we've collected on our travels. Again, Diane the Decider helps it all go from hodge-podge to happily-ever-after looks.

Q: Do you have a favorite piece of furniture that resonates with you like my multiple dining tables?
Carolanne: Could it be the antique French Country dining room table Johnny found one Thanksgiving Eve and had moved into the lake house as the sun set. It now serves as a gathering place for family, company, buffets featuring dish after dish, and sit-down meals any time of day. On that late November Wednesday I greeted the notion of the new table with a groan—I'd already fully set the existing table down to the last perfectly-placed pumpkin and carefully folded napkin—and wasn't keen on re-doing the whole thing. It arrived, I fell in love, and Johnny became the holiday's hero.

As for decor "moments," I'd add the Standard Talking Machine Company "Victrola" complete with playable records from around 1904 (it's like a couch-side sculpture with history); or the beautiful holiday tree on the mantle, created by my mother decades ago from carefully-folded tissue paper sprayed gold. You must see to believe but it's priceless—just as she was.

Two Dog Night

When the thermometer hits anywhere below 60 degrees, it's officially winter here in Florida. Nothing excites a sunshine state resident more than the opportunity to turn on the heat and pull out the wool winter coat with the price tag still on. A light watery sheet of ice topped my car today and I was downright giddy. Mind you, I'm only in this for a few days before dreaming of sunny days at the beach that command a few droplets of sweat. I'm a bonafide winter wimp.

Our LhasaPoo pups—Lucy and Lizzy—are conditioned to be the same way, bless 'em. A few hard-freeze days with their tender paws touching cold crunchy grass sends them straight back into the house. Alas, bedtime means they end up firmly snuggled on top of a soft blanket on our bed, Lucy right next to Mike and Lizzy cupped into the arc of my stomach as I sleep on my side.

When we moved into this house, we bought a king-sized bed, our first. Tonight, Mike is on the far-right side clinging for life. My legs are numb hanging on the other side. Our precious pups have claimed their rightly-deserved territory. We had more space with two toddlers in a full bed on those nights the ghosts appeared in their rooms propelling them to mom and dad's bed. Alas, here we are, a married couple with two dogs in a bed just waiting for a New Yorker cartoon to be composed about us.

"'Night, honey," I say stretching my hand to find my husband.

"G'Night, sweetie," he says as his fingertips stretch to touch mine.

Ain't life grand?

SET YOUR TABLE

Animals are love. Find one. Love one. Grant them space on the bed. Just make it king-sized.

I Must Dance

My daughter's friend Alia got married. Gilly texted pics to me. There's a photo of us two on the dance floor, our favorite location. 'Tis the season for my children's friends getting married and I am all in for it. How gratifying to see my children-by-love find happiness, be it at the altar, new job, new home, new hobby. And when a special occasion includes a DJ, Mike knows to find me cutting a rug with the young folk.

I try not to embarrass myself, cue Elaine from Seinfeld, and there's a few dances I refuse to do like the Macarena. Que soy bueno? No lo creo. Line dances are also off limits. Gimme room to bust a move, people! Honestly, I'm just thrilled to be invited and hope the bride and groom don't have invitation remorse.

In between weddings, I'm known to take a spin around the kitchen island with my very own disco ball. Off season requires a disciplined regimen of training. My Dance Coach Dua Lipa agrees. I believe dancing is one of the best ways to be fully present in the moment, in the music, so own it. So, sayeth Eminem, "You better lose yourself in the music."

SET YOUR TABLE

Create a playlist of your top five favorite dance-worthy tunes. Dance like no one is watching because, well, they usually aren't.

Hot Time in the Studio

By an act of impetuousness, I signed up for hot yoga. Not sure how this happened. Thought I clicked to order hot chocolate online and ended up with my elbows to ears at a local studio. This is the month of restarts. However, I can't really resume something I never began. Yet, there I was, in an infrared room the size of a small bedroom next to Yoga classmates whose bones were made of rubber.

I managed to keep up with the 100 different poses. Then our instructor told us to pull out the yoga blocks, a hard foam brick used for torturing out-of-shape humans. Allegedly, the blocks are used to help difficult poses be more accessible and develop strength. I developed a neck ache.

"Here, try this," the instructor said bending down to adjust my head, "Relax and lean into your inner light."

The pose called for my left arm to be positioned above my head which was turned the opposite direction as I laid, stomach down, on the mat, all while propping my head on the block of hell.

When class ended, I wobbled outside, bowing to the divine Hyundai SUV that would usher me away. Namaste, mother blockers!

A few days later, I returned to the studio because winners never quit and the muscle spasms stopped. This time I brought my own damn block which was really a decorative pillow from my living room sofa. Much better! And to think all I needed to do was lean into my living room.

SET YOUR TABLE

Yoga tip: pillows are better than blocks. You're welcome.

Favorite Find: Wall of Love

What to do when you have more photos than wall space? MixTile it! This is not a paid endorsement unless the online print store is looking for a new influencer whose followers are family, friends and resident dogs. The 8x8 inch photos, aka "tiles," are removable, reusable and don't leave a mark. And so easy to order! Turn on the app and upload your favorite cell phone photos.

I've lined up a hallway with what I call my "Wall of Love," MixTile pics of memories worth preserving. Each time I pass by, I feel the warmth of gratitude to have my beloveds close by. When I add a new tile, I'll snap a picture of it on my cell—yes, a phone pic of a phone pic, go figure—and share it with the star of the new tile. Stephen, my nephew-by-love, said he forwarded my message to his friends who were also in the tile pic, a snapshot of a fun wedding rehearsal get-together.

"Hey, we made Aunt Amy's wall of love!" he texted.

Yes, you did. And there's plenty more wall space waiting to be honored.

SET YOUR TABLE

Find a neglected wall, order a MixTile. Savor the memory. Repeat.

Poppyseed Ministry

When someone is going through a difficult time, I activate what I call my Poppyseed Ministry—delivery of love in the form of comfort food, my Poppyseed Chicken Casserole. I keep a staple of ingredients in my pantry complete with disposable foil pans so I can make, bake and drop off in just a few hours' notice. Sometimes I make extra to store in the freezer for convenience and, of course, an extra dish for Mike! When the kiddos come home to visit, this is often their meal request.

AMY'S POPPYSEED CHICKEN CASSEROLE

INGREDIENTS

2 packages of noodles (I prefer spinach noodle nests, but any kind will do.)
2 tablespoons olive oil
2 ½ pounds of thick-sliced deli chicken breasts cut into bite-size pieces, (about 6 cups)
2 10½ oz. of cream of chicken soup
1 ½ cups sour cream
1 can sliced water chestnuts. (I love 'em so I add two cans.)
1 teaspoon dried tarragon leaves
½ teaspoon pepper and salt
1 cup crumbled Ritz crackers (I use more for pure yumminess and crunch)
2 teaspoons poppyseed
6 tablespoons melted butter

DIRECTIONS

- In large saucepan, cook noodles according to package.
- Drain and toss with olive oil.
- Place noodles in two 7 x 11 inch pans.
- In a medium bowl, combine the chicken, soup, sour cream, water chestnuts, tarragon and salt and pepper
- Pour soup mixture over noodles.
- Sprinkle the cracker crumbs and poppyseed over mixture.
- Pour melted butter over crackers.
- Bake uncovered in a pre-heated 325-degree oven for 30-40 minutes.

SET YOUR TABLE

Create your own ministry of love with a gift that soothes the soul and stomach.

Camellia

For the life of me, I don't understand why any flower blooms during the cold winter. Yet, my backyard is awash in pink camellias just in time for Valentine's Day. Grabbing a pair of garden shears, also known as craft scissors in my house, I clip a few beautiful blooms to showcase inside. I discovered that placing them in petite white vases complements their beauty. My design tendencies tend more inside than out, so I've enjoyed exploring combining the two. Just don't tell Martha Stewart about the craft scissors.

SET YOUR TABLE

Bring a little floral jewelry inside to brighten your chilly day.

March

Centerpieces: Listen

With Spring around the corner, it's easy to fall into a flurry of activity, shedding winter's hibernation for repeated runs to Home Depot. Resist the impulse, at least long enough to turn off the car. Instead, stop and listen to what I've come to call the tender bridge between resting and running.

I like to use the last week of March as my pause button. Sometimes this means simply being still. Mostly, I just listen. To myself. I got a lot going on in this little brain of mine. *Too* much. Warmer weather and sunnier skies invigorate me to get out and do more. I once created project lists for home renovations, writing, my body, work, reading, learning. Did I mention my body? No. More. Pasta. Then, I combine the lists into one master document, print all 100 pages and crawl beneath the covers overwhelmed by it all, usually with a big bowl of fettuccine.

Enough.

I discovered when I let go of the urge to fill up the extra hours of light, I let in something brighter—permission to be open to unplanned possibilities. This means listening to the cadence of my internal barometer, which rarely leads me astray. It's like I have Mister Rogers on repeat in my amygdala. Some days bring high vibes, others low, so, I respond accordingly. Home Depot need not worry. Soon, the universe and my limbic system will be in alignment and I'll be open to what the moment decrees.

SET YOUR TABLE

Hit your pause button to listen and learn from an emotional expert—you.

The Girl Wore Prada

I once visited the Fetzer Institute in Kalamazoo, Michigan in the dead of winter for a workshop based on the work of noted inspirational educator and author Parker Palmer. As a thin-skinned Floridian, I felt a rush of cool air the minute I booked the flight. And the minute I landed, I came down with an actual cold, the runny, red-chapped nose and sneezing kind. Exactly what none of my workshop participants wanted to be around.

The saving grace was that my friend Pat joined me. Aside from being one of the smartest people I know, she is one of the most gracious. Where others feared to tread, Pat loaded me up with Kleenex, hot tea, the new Anna Quindlen book, and a command to stay in my room until I felt better. Outside the impressive campus the snow blanketed a forest of sparse trees. It was stunningly beguiling, and I was stunningly bummed not to be at the workshop. So I downed some Dayquil, stuffed tissues in the pockets of my black wool coat from Sam's Wholesale, and headed toward the main building.

My classmates represented a diverse group of education professionals including the executive director of the Lyndon Baines Johnson Presidential Museum. She carried herself like Grace Kelly, drenched in elegance and a luxurious wool coat, definitely not from a big box store. To be honest, I was intimidated sitting next to her and did everything I could not to cough in her direction. Eventually, the cold medicine wore off and I was a miserable sack.

I retreated back to my room, ready for a steam shower and bed. A few hours later, Pat knocked on my door with a half-smile.

"Hey, kiddo," Pat said as she handed me what looked like a coat, "Apparently, you and Miss LBJ took each other's coats. She pulled out her room key and, instead, held a wad of limp tissues."

Mortified, I grabbed the stolen frock on the bed and handed it to Pat to return the designer coat back to its rightful, and healthy, owner.

Later in the week, when I felt better and believed I would live to see another day, Pat and I shared a nice bottle of Chardonnay reliving what happened. That's when I realized this—true friends show up and make you feel a little less vulnerable, a little more loved. Which was just what I needed on that chilly Michigan night when LBJ mistook a Kleenex for a key and Snotty-Nosed Girl wore Prada.

SET YOUR TABLE

Laugh at yourself. Find someone who will, too, and loves you anyway, tissues and all.

@RothRetzArtist

A MOMENT WITH

Cass Roth Retz

"To me, home is recharging, relaxing and creating a place the outside world can't invade!"

Well said, Cass Roth Retz, interior decorator extraordinaire in New York City. I've known this brilliant human since, well, forever. She may live in New York City, but she hails from Ocala, Florida.

Amy Mangan

Our families have a deep and true connection growing up in a small Southern town. I've watched her grow into an insanely talented artist. Whatever she does, she pursues it with panache. Cass sources much of her inspiration from living in New York City – "Whether it's a beautiful brownstone, an amazing painting in a museum or a 20-something hipster on the train in a super retro outfit, inspiration and clever is everywhere!"

Q: What is your favorite kind of space to design?
Cass: Each project brings new and interesting challenges. I have worked on ballrooms to boardrooms and they are all equally challenging and interesting in their own right as are the clients who live in them.

Q: Do you have a sentimental accent piece?
Cass: I'm in love with this vintage photo of the George Washington Bridge taken from the Cloisters, circa 1962 in the living room. I swiped it from my mom's house the last time I made a Florida visit. I will also never part with my bespoke antique bar I created from a shell of a Swedish cabinet purchased in New Orleans years ago. I have collected vintage barware for years. Let's just say I have a tiny issue. My favorite will always be my grandmother's pieces she lovingly gave to me over the years. The funniest story was when the movers arrived to my first NYC apartment, they refused to carry it up the four flights of stairs because it wouldn't fit in the elevator. You have never seen a crazier Southern girl on the streets of NYC. Needless to say, the cabinet made it into the apartment.

SET YOUR TABLE

Designers like Cass remind us to lift up sentimental heirlooms to their rightful spot in our homes.

WATCH LIST:
All Creatures Great and Small

I interrupt this book to share a television show recommendation. When I was young, my father, an avid reader, gave me a copy of James Herriot's *All Creatures Great and Small*. He suggested we add this to our Sunday afternoon father-daughter reading. Halfway through the heartfelt memoir of a country vet in England I realized Dad had already read it. I could see why—it was hard not to fall in love with the quirky villagers and their animals. The current television series is the perfect antidote to all the world's craziness, inviting you to take a break and sip a cuppa tea.

SET YOUR TABLE

Watch the remake of All Creatures Great and Small on PBS. Tears and laughter guaranteed.

Obituary

The start of my day includes reading obituaries, a ritual that began after the September 11 attacks. I committed to read what would formally become the New York Times' series "Portraits of Grief." Poignant and heartbreaking, I was struck by the common themes throughout each profile. They were everyday Americans going about their lives as mothers, sons, firefighters, managers, car enthusiasts, chefs, investment bankers, community volunteers, little league coaches.

Humans.

Since then, I've added a few more newspapers to my reading collection. Vivid pictures of remembrances come into focus. Harold the trumpet player who won over his future wife with a rousing solo of The Beatles' "All You Need is Love." Eve's post-retirement travel adventures across Europe. A special edition Ford Thunderbird made it in ink for Bob who apparently loved his wife and the car they bought together in equal measure.

Each week the Wall Street Journal highlights a few deceased business leaders who typically overcame adversity, career changes, mediocre grades in high school and early work failures to reach success. I read those, too.

Growing up, Sunday lunches at my parents' home inevitably turned into conversations about who died. "Did you see that Janice's husband, Tom, passed? Wasn't he related to the Smith family who owned the local car dealership? No, that was his cousin who was married to Elaine and they sold the business to retire up North to be with their kids. Amy, I think you went to school with one of them. No, Mama, that was Cindy who went to middle school with their oldest." Twenty minutes later, we had covered an extensive geography of minutia and everyone had forgotten about poor Tom.

Now I catch myself doing the same thing with Mike, so reading about strangers limits the impulse. However, since I'm one of the last living Americans who subscribe to the print edition of newspapers, I feel it's my duty to keep friends and family informed. Mostly, though, I read obituaries because I find them to be powerful prompts to stay centered in who and what truly matters. I've yet to read a profile where the departed dedicated his or her life to checking off every action item on the calendar or staying late one more hour to finish an email. Give me trumpets, Italy, and T-birds any day.

SET YOUR TABLE

Take a minute to read an obituary, honoring the departed and respecting the beauty of the living.

'Nati Nights

I'm not a Cincinnati Reds fan, but my friend, Heather, is. It doesn't hurt she lives close by the Reds' stadium. When I visited her, she gave me this coaster. She also introduced me to Graeter's ice cream so I love her forever.

The coaster sits on my bedside table reminding me of a fun visit when my work colleagues and I toured 'Nati—as the locals say—and crossed the state line to Kentucky in Heather's four-seat car with six of us packed in like a clown troop. And whooping it up like little kids when we reached Kentucky. The trip took all of 10 minutes. Who'd of thunk? We indulged in the city's famous chili and ate copious amounts of black raspberry chocolate chip ice cream.

Sometimes I stress over the right gift for friends. Then I look at my coaster. And think of Heather, our clown car voyage and how I can convince Graeter's to open an Ocala store. A gift means so much more than itself.

SET YOUR TABLE

What is a gift that takes you down memory lane?

What's In a Name

St. Patrick's Day puts me on a guilt trip and not because I'm Irish or Catholic. I'm neither, which is a shame as this would kind of explain the self-inflicted guilt. And while I'm embarrassed by the commercialization of the Irish's sacred holiday—no, the patron saint of Ireland did not drink green beer and dress like a leprechaun—I can cut our green-clad friends some slack. What gets me about this day is that it reminds me I've been a negligent mother.

I married into an Irish family, the Mangans. I have now shared the extent of my knowledge about my children's Irish roots. My side of the family, the Yearys, hailed from Scotland, what part I do not know. The part where it's cold, I think.

Through the years, I've intended to read through some of our personal history researched and compiled by other family members. When St. Patrick's Day rolls around, it usually prompts my children to ask about their heritage. I tell them they are Scotch-Irish and then give them shamrock shirts I bought at Target. However, my daughter is taking a children's literature class in college, and the professor assigned a personal folklore project. She asked me if we have an Irish family story. Go ask your dad, I told her.

Okay, Gillian, this much I know:

Your dad, Michael George Mangan, was born with a good Irish name as was his sister, Theresa Ann, and brother Patrick James. Their father, George Francis, raised his sons as practicing altar boys in their Catholic school and church. Their Uncle Jimmy, James Joseph Mangan, visited Ireland once and returned with copies of the Mangan crest for everyone. As far as family crests go, it's not the worst, but not the best. The center of the crest bears a hand with two circles above it and a crescent shield beneath like something you'd see in law enforcement, which could come in handy if you're pulled over by a police officer, but only if he's an Irish cop.

The Mangan name is the Anglicized form of the Gaelic O Mongain, meaning a descendant of Mongan. It was originally a byname for someone with a luxuriant head of hair, a thick "mane," which explains your dad and uncle's thick, wavy hair. Most of the original Mangans were born in Connacht, County Limerick. Once, your dad and I visited the local Catholic priest in his church office. He pulled out a large book about Ireland and showed us beautiful photos of the County Limerick, home of "many a Mangan," he said.

We have a famous writer on your dad's side of the family, James Clarence Mangan, a Dublin-born poet in the early 19th century. James Joyce and William Butler Yeats considered Mangan one of the best Irish poets, so you get your love of verse naturally.

Your dad will share with you the time your Papa George and Uncle Jimmy were reunited as young soldiers fighting at the Battle of Anzio in Italy in World War II. The brothers were in separate army divisions. George found his little brother in the valley and got him a hot meal and shower. Jimmy returned to his battalion and was later wounded in the battle, yet, survived. Both brothers spoke often about what it meant to find each other during war.

I also know this: a family name only means something when there is love that defines it, a bond that keeps us together through good and difficult times. And you and your brother have that in spades, or rather shamrocks, something worth celebrating every day of the year.

SET YOUR TABLE

Honor someone Irish in your life or, go to a pub and buy a pint of Guinness for a lad or lassie.

April

Centerpieces: Grace

A new keepsake: I purchased this sweet piece of pottery from a Brooklyn artist. While walking with Gilly from lunch in Greenpoint, we turned the corner to see a pop-up shop of ceramic creations. Gilly and I both selected the same small bowl, giddy over our inexpensive find. Mine is nestled on the corner of my home office desk next to the front porch window. Along with a candle, it sits atop a small tray with a rendering of the landmark Greenbrier Resort, another keepsake from another memorable trip. I use the bowl to keep daily inspiration cards.

Each morning before I tackle what's in front of me, I light the candle, read an inspiration, then pray. The ritual takes all of five minutes and when I skip a morning, I miss it, and I make sure not to the next day. And when the rest of the day clutters my workflow and mind, I simply look across the desk to see my little Zen tableau. Grace in a bowl.

SET YOUR TABLE

Create a comfort ritual to honor loved keepsakes and people, including yourself.

Some Bunny Loves You

I love celebrations, a genetic disposition inherited from my mother who honored all holidays, birthdays, anniversaries and any random occasion in between. Growing up in Mama's house meant family members were required to obtain a degree from Nel Yeary's Event Decorating and Themed Appetizer School. You know it's bad when your garage is full of storage totes labeled for St. Patrick's Day, a minor calendar event in a home of Anglican genealogy. We're not Irish, but that didn't stop Mama from baking green shamrock-shaped blueberry muffins which, once you got past the lime green food coloring, were, actually, quite tasty.

Mom's move into an assisted-living facility resulted in a serious paring down of her lifelong party décor collection. This is where four daughters come in. My sisters and I kept some of her special mementos, proudly displaying them in our respective homes when the right holiday rolls around. Well, that's not entirely true. I possess, but do not display, Mom's voice-activated door décor Easter Bunny that, upon a door's opening, screeches in a Jack Nicholson-meets-an-overcaffeinated-Bugs Bunny voice, "Heeeeeeeey, Some Bunny Loves You!" It scared the children when they were little, not to mention my husband who is still adjusting to the fact his mother-in-law once owned musical Easter egg salt and pepper shakers that played Irving Berlin's "The Easter Parade." (The pepper shaker always was stuck on the first verse though a firm wrist shake could easily remedy the problem.)

Of course, fashion accompanied the fanfare. Mom owned enough costume and holiday-themed jewelry to fill a small warehouse. Her style was a cross between Liberace and Lady Gaga. The more bling, the better… especially if it was shaped like a Christmas tree. You can only imagine Mom's elation when her middle-school-aged daughter informed her she was going to be in a play about the American Revolution. Before sundown, Mama had whipped out her sewing machine and created a red, white and blue long dress and kerchief. I'm not sure how many of our founding fathers and mothers wore kerchiefs, but I wore mine with patriotic pride. Never mind the fact my dress was made from one of Mom's Fourth of July tablecloths. Ketchup stains added a raw kind of panache to my style. So, there, George Washington!

Decades went by when I vowed to be a holiday minimalist. A tasteful boxwood wreath on the door sufficed on most occasions. Then, I thought of the screeching bunnies, musical food condiment accessories, and Little Miss Revolution Haute Couture. Who am I kidding? No one smiles at boxwoods. Order ye' up some singing bunnies and let's see where that takes us. I'd like to think it's somewhere Mama would love.

SET YOUR TABLE

Make Nelwyn proud — decorate with bunny abandon.

Food Coordinator

Eggs seem to be the healing salve between hurt and hope. Egg salad. Egg casserole. Deviled eggs—especially deviled eggs which have a way of shifting the too-gray conversation to something much lighter. But that may be a matter of whether the recipe calls for whipped or low-fat mayonnaise. And is paprika necessary? Having weaved in and out of heartache that comes with the territory of living, I can fully attest that, in many ways, analyzing the texture of an egg salad sandwich bridged me from dark uncertainty to a brighter and much-needed respite.

In the mercurial rotation of life, food is the pre-eminent stabilizer. The circumstances of both my children's births reinforced the power of comfort food. Stumbling in late each night after visiting our first-born premature baby in a teaching hospital 45 minutes away, my husband and I were greeted by a warm meal sitting on our kitchen counter. Friends and family made sure dinner was waiting so we'd have one less thing to think about. When I found myself on three-months of bed rest while pregnant with my daughter, the food patrol arrived, once again, often staying to sit awhile, helping me pass the time over a bowl of homemade soup.

Recently, a close friend suffered both a personal loss and an unexpected health crisis. As I walked through her kitchen, foil-covered casseroles and sealed desserts were neatly stacked on the table, reminding me of the beauty of community. My friend was struck by this generosity, too. Through the fog of fatigue and sadness, she smiled and said, "I have arrived—I have my own food coordinator!"

A pot of green beans can't erase the raw reality, but it can dull the pain as if to say, "We're in this together."

Comfort food's unspoken code reinforces fellowship's selfless gesture. I've learned the value of preparing meals in disposable dishes and remembering little ones by making kid-friendly dinners as well (when in doubt, do pizza.) Plus, there's no harm in tossing a mindless magazine or two into the food basket (permission granted to dwell on the mundane matters of a fading pop-star celebrity). And, perhaps most importantly, it is understood that gratitude doesn't require formal correspondence. When bringing me dinner one night, a friend said, "Do not write me a thank you note. I know you appreciate this and I appreciate being able to do this for you."

The gift of emotional nourishment is a two-way street, providing edible compassion to someone who's hurting while making the rest of us feel like we're doing something of modest help. Who knew the healing powers of pound cake? When nothing else can be said or done, a slice of cake is often the most reassuring antidote for both the giver and receiver.

Memories fade in and out on the day my nephew died. One clear image reappears—that of two friends walking through my door carrying coolers of iced bottled water, paper plates, and fried chicken with deviled eggs. They shuffled about in my kitchen, unpacking their goods while I sat on the back porch surveying a plate of food in front of me. The eggs were dusted with paprika.

For a moment, I felt like I could breathe again

SET YOUR TABLE

Nourish someone's soul and heart this week.

Bedside Notes

Before memory failed me, remembering things came easily. While I cannot pinpoint the exact date of this memory loss—a classic symptom of cantus rememberus squatus—it began sometime in my early 30s, coinciding with my children's births, known as placenta de brain drainus. Today, my ability to recall even the most insignificant items remains elusive, punctuated by moments of enlightenment at bedtime. As a result, I keep a notepad and pen handy by my bed so when Mother Insight visits, I'm ready.

For some reason, thoughts pop into my head upon impact with a pillow. It's as though a synapse suddenly clicks, sending a flood of information to a previously deprived neuron. To wit—while reading James Joyce, I remember I need to pick up the dry cleaning. The connection? Oh, a day in Dublin! Gotta get those starched shirts! And just as that dream begins about John Travolta sitting in my history class, CLICK, I realize I forgot to return an important phone call. These moments of lucidity are clouded by absolute randomness, making my hastily scribbled notes read as a fragmented journal entry, like Martha Stewart on too much caffeine. Call Sheila for lunch! Buy milk! Charge cell phone! Edit column! Toilet paper! Grade papers! Put clothes in dryer! Pine Nuts!

Other notes reveal dimmer mental snippets requiring an expert code breaker on par with World War II Allied Powers. "BLT money" means I need to pay the tuition for my daughter's ballet class. Or do I just need a bacon, lettuce and tomato sandwich? "Plug" reminds me to charge the video camera. "Pics" suggests putting out clean shirts for the children to wear on picture day which is always a good idea. Sometimes even I can't figure out what I wrote, an especially scary thought when three exclamation points follow the inscription. This is why writing in the dark is discouraged. One morning I awoke to find "Need toilet paper!!!" etched upon the cover of my favorite Pat Conroy book.

I'm sorry, Pat. If I had gone just three more inches, I'd have made it to the notepad. No one ever writes on my books, not even me, buddy.

The lowest point came last week when I jotted some one word notations—"Food!!!" Decoded: pull something out of the freezer to fix for dinner. "Children!!!" Translation: pick them up at early release from school. I placed this last note on my car window just to be safe.

It's getting worse. I now have notepads in my car, by each phone, even by the washer and dryer. My home is decorated in French Country sticky notes. It's an unusual wall covering choice to be sure.

Technology has lessened the symptoms somewhat so. Occasionally, I'll send myself an email, but that works only if I remember to check my email. See how complicated this is getting? I make notes to remember to check my notes

A hundred years from now, I envision an archaeological team standing over what use to be my home. They'll pick at a faded yellow scrap buried deep in the earth. Looking more closely, they'll squint to read the incoherent etching on the document.

"Ah yes, we have found an artifact used to enhance the cognitive development of the 21st century American woman," says the archaeologist. "This tool provided a way to maximize time for the American family. Children were fed. Husbands made appointments on time. Corporations ran more efficiently. The only apparent downside was a noted change in sleep patterns of many women found sleeping while clutching a small clump of paper."

SET YOUR TABLE

Be specific with your notetaking or else you'll wind up with too many pine nuts and not enough toilet paper.

Gimlets and Checklists

Past moves have typically gone like this:
　　Garage sale complete. Check.
　　Packing complete. Check.
Celebratory gimlet martini. Check.
Incredible sisters Cindy and Julie who organized the entire sale and move. Double check.
Husband who tolerates my book addiction as he moves heavy boxes from one home to the next. Check.
Friend Mary showing up before sunrise in pouring rain with a Diet Coke. What a beautiful soul. Check.
Post-move Gimlet to celebrate. Check.
Lucky to be loved by giving humans? Oh, yeah.

REASON TO CELEBRATE ANYTHING GIMLET

INGREDIENTS

2 oz. vodka
¾ oz. lime juice, freshly squeezed
½ oz. simple syrup (or Stevia as a sugar-free option)
Lime wheel

DIRECTIONS

- Freeze martini glass in advance.
- Add the vodka, lime juice and simple syrup into a shaker with ice and shake until well-chilled.
- Strain into chilled glass.
- Garnish with the lime wheel.

SET YOUR TABLE

Make a toast in honor of friends and family.

@ByErinSparks

A MOMENT WITH

Erin Sparks

Meet Erin Sparks whose specialty is finding a balance between expensive items with budget-friendly ones and antiques with more modern pieces.

Amy Mangan

"I like the feel of intimacy that comes with small spaces..."

Q: What is your favorite kind of space to design?
Erin: I enjoy working with small spaces the most. I like the feel of intimacy that comes with small spaces such as a reading nook or small office.

Q: Do you have a current accent piece that's a favorite?
Erin: My dining room drapery trim — I'm in love with it! This little beaded detail just makes me so happy!

Q: What does home mean to you?
Erin: Home is a comfort zone and a safe haven where I am free to express my creativity and experiment in design without judgment. I see my home as an ongoing project where I can embrace imperfection and enjoy the journey of creating something beautiful to live in for my family.

Q: Anything else you'd like to include about yourself?
Erin: My sweet spot is lighting. I am in love with light fixtures, and I think lighting can make or break a room. This is usually where I splurge!

SET YOUR TABLE

Remember to include beautiful lighting as the jewelry for a room.

Spoiling With Love

I lost my mother on an early morning in late April, a day that was vividly drenched in spring's sunlight as if Mama had lit the sky with her radiance. A few days prior, in between nursing home shifts shared with my sisters, I wrote her obituary sensing the end was near. The end result was the first and only writing I've ever drafted without revising. It was if Mama was writing it for me, which, in a way, she was.

Nelwyn "Nel" Yeary was reunited in Heaven with her beloved husband, Sherman Yeary, Jr. on Thursday, April 29, 2021.

Born a Southern lady in Lyons, Georgia on July 12, 1925, Nel and her family soon moved to Ocala, Florida. It was here where Nel met Sherman and asked him out on their first date at the Second Baptist Church's Girls in Action banquet. It was love at first sight and, years later, they married after Sherman returned home from serving abroad in World War II.

They raised four daughters who proudly loved being known as the "Yeary girls"—Donna, Julie, Cindy and Amy. Their Mama was proud, too, and enjoyed dressing her girls in beautiful hand-sewn dresses and cooking delicious Southern comfort food for her family, friends and, usually, half of Ocala. Her home became the gathering spot for church parties, engagement dinners, bridal and baby showers and all major and minor holidays. She always had her famous pistachio cake waiting on the kitchen counter and a freezer full of homemade chocolate ice cream parfaits.

Then the grandchildren came and Nel was in her full caregiving element ascending to her new favorite title as Mamaw. Gidget, Holly, Josh, Molly, Valori, Lisa, Griffin and Gillian spent many a day and night playing in Mamaw's laundry and sewing room which also served as toy central for eager grandkids.

If ever someone told Nel she was spoiling her children and grandchildren, she quickly responded "I just spoil them with love!" Boy, did she.

As if she didn't stay busy enough caring for her expanding family and decorating one Sherman Yeary-built home after another, Nel became a successful real estate agent and broker, eventually running ABC Realty then working at Roberts Real Estate, where she made long-lasting friendships with an impressive portfolio of real estate transactions.

She leaves a legacy of love to her family—her children, Donna Grubbs (Roddy), Julie Moody (Stanley, deceased), Cindy Fleetwood (Brad) and Amy Mangan (Mike), her grandchildren Gidget Lewis, Holly Ignatz, Molly Moody, Joshua Moody (deceased), Valori Hall, Lisa Lewis, Gillian and Griffin Mangan and 11 great-grandchildren. Deceased before her were parents, Lola and H.A. Odom, and sister Clovis Brack (George, Sr.). Clovis and George's son, George, Jr. (Buddy, married to Judy), has remained a cherished nephew who visited Nel weekly.

A private family service will be held. There will not be a visitation, however, donations in honor of Nel may be made to the Skills Day Center, Inc., P.O Box 5652, Ocala, Florida 34478 and Interfaith Emergency Services, P.O. Box 992, Ocala, Florida 34478.

The family requests you celebrate Nel with a good Southern meal with your loved ones. Be sure to include her favorite dishes she was known for—fresh pole beans, a pot roast marinated in Italian dressing, squash casserole, mashed potatoes with gravy, sweet tea (the sweeter the better), Libby's biscuits and, of course, a pistachio cake.

We'd like to believe Mama is making this very meal for Sherman and most of Heaven right now.

SET YOUR TABLE

Spoil your family with love and cook up a mouth-watering Southern meal, sweet tea included. Pistachio Cake, an added bonus.

Slow Down, Honey

After Mama passed, my friend Dorothy gave me a set of wind chimes with engraved with "I just spoil them with love"—the absolute perfect gift, so much, in fact, I now give inscribed wind chimes to others after the loss of a loved one. My chimes hang above the rocking chairs on our front porch. Each day when I go in and out of my home, I'm greeted by Mama. Sometimes, when I'm fumbling for my keys to open the front door in a hurry, I hear the most melodic chimes ring as if Mama is saying "Slow down, honey. You'll eventually get to where you need to be."

SET YOUR TABLE

Notes, flowers and casseroles are good, but a personal touch with customized wind chimes offer a poignant way to remember and honor.

May

Centerpieces: Adjust

Hard to believe we're almost halfway through the year. This is the month when I spend a good bit of time framing where I've been and where I want to be. It's my check and adjust season, tweaking plans and dreams to stay on course. However, sometimes the course is the very thing that needs editing. With winter in my rearview mirror, I'm invigorated by the notion of renewal. I'm also motivated that swimsuit season is tapping on my doughy shoulders, reminding me to dust off the weights in my closet.

SET YOUR TABLE

As we move into summer, let's resolve to revive our resolutions and remove those that are no longer useful. Time for a fresh start!

What May Come and Go, Some Things Will Remain

A chronic mover, I've thought a lot about the things I've kept, packed, unpacked and re-packed.

Some of my keepable items make sense—photo albums, coffee maker, packing boxes. But I've held on to a few others for reasons that yield more sentiment than sense. Like the chipped ceramic bowl given to me by a close friend. Or the brass anniversary clock whose pendulum rotates only when placed at just the right angle on a sunny day. "Gee Gee," our adopted family caregiver who has since passed, gave this to me so it's a keeper. I get this from Mama whose health mandated a season of downsizing, but she clung to one special item she would not part with.

Mom grew up in an impoverished setting, a repercussion from the Great Depression. Electricity, plumbing and secure shelter were considered luxuries for her family. The actress Shirley Temple was popular when mom was a little girl. Temple rose to fame at the tender age of 6 when she starred in "Bright Eyes," a film designed for her talents of singing, dancing and being adorable. She was mom's peer, just two years younger, and inspired little girls across the world with her iconic innocence.

The Shirley Temple doll, complete with tight-brown curls and a red polka dot tulle dress, was all the rage. Mom wanted one so badly. She said she would walk by the department store and look at the doll in the window.

"Oh my goodness! What I wouldn't give to have that doll," she'd often say. But she knew a doll wasn't an option for her family who could barely afford the basic staples of living.

She also knew college was out of the question. Instead, she used her high school straight-A smarts to work part-time at different jobs while raising a family of four daughters and helping my father, a World War II vet, to start and grow his construction business. I was her youngest daughter, and when

I reached high school, mom earned her real estate license and thrived. By my senior year, she earned her real estate broker's license at 57 years old.

She also received a gift from Dad to celebrate: her very own Shirley Temple doll. He ordered it from a catalog and cautioned her to keep it in the box to preserve its value. Mom tore that box open like a kid on Christmas morning and placed her doll in its stand on the dining room buffet for all to see.

The doll stayed with mom through many changes—owning a real estate agency, watching her daughters pave their own paths, enjoying grandchildren (who would carefully play with the doll under mom's careful eye), managing dad's chronic illness and passing, and, eventually, facing her own illness and subsequent move from her home to assisted living.

Shirley the doll had been with her through it all.

Shirley the woman redefined her life, moving from child star to an accomplished diplomat including service as the United States Ambassador to Ghana. She underplayed her impact as an actress, saying, "People in the Depression wanted something to cheer them up, and they fell in love with a dog and a little girl."

Mom fell in love with what Shirley Temple meant to her—someone full of life, hope and the promise of something good and pure. Her dimpled doll held command on the top of a bookshelf near her bed. Though fragile in the twilight of her life, mom looked up with knowing clarity, smiling with bright eyes.

And, now, so will I.

SET YOUR TABLE

Try not to discard a beloved's heirlooms because they are your own treasured memory.

Of Mandolins and Memories

Several years ago, Mike and I took the kids to Jacksonville to see Garrison Keillor's "A Prairie Home Companion" live show, which is when I came to appreciate the spell-bounding powers of a mandolin.

Keillor introduced guest performer Peter Oshtroushko on stage to "play a tune for the fine folks" on his mandolin. Oshtroushko nestled the teardrop string instrument close to his body, then, bowing his head, paused for seconds that felt like minutes as if to say grace for what was about to happen, with no regard for the pregnant silence in the packed auditorium.

Mercifully, he began to play. Tenderly plucking the strings to create a haunting, melodic sound, this mandolin player I'd never heard of before taught me what magic sounds like. He strummed his original composition "Puckett's Farewell," a tender homage to the late baseball Hall of Famer Kirby Puckett, but, truly, I felt he was playing for me.

We drove back to our hotel sensing the earth moved, or, at least the northern part of Florida shifted a little. Even at 10 and 8 years old, Griffin and Gillian seemed to recognize we had witnessed something special. Many a Saturday night afterward, at 6 p.m., we'd find ourselves on our back porch sharing two chaises while listening to Keillor's radio show.

A lot has happened since that trip, but the mandolin has remained one of my favorite musical instruments. And "A Prairie Home Companion" has never disappointed. When I can, I turn on the show, now usually via my cell phone app or car satellite radio. But time stands still for no one or radio show, including Keillor. In July, he retired from the show he created. Chris Thile assumed his role for a blissful period.

Ironically, Thile is an accomplished mandolin player. I was first introduced to Thile when he played in a four-string ensemble with cellist Yo-Yo Ma and have been a fan ever since. Still, Thile had big shoes to fill. I imagine he'd bring his own millennial pair to wear, lending a new sound and style to the show that once captured the hearts of a young family from Ocala.

Mike and I are now the parents of young adults who live in two different cities away from their parents. Most days, I've come to terms with this empty nest chapter; other times, not so much. I think I've struck a healthy emotional balance except for when I hear a mandolin play or find an old episode of the one and only radio show that ever caused my world to stop for just a little blissful while. Then I get misty.

Oh, what I'd give to have just one evening to be back on the porch of my former home with my children as we squeezed a family of four and a puppy onto a seat made for two. But, thus far, I've been unable to secure a time machine on Amazon.com. So, I'll have to settle for the memories made on those magical Saturday nights.

Thile appeared in an Ocala concert with Effie O'Donavan recently. When he gently plucked the first mandolin strings, I was taken back on the outdoor porch with my family curled up on a too-small chaise lounge.

And it was wonderful.

SET YOUR TABLE

Creating meaningful experiences with loved ones is always a priority for me. What is yours? Go forth and create some.

Signs of Leaf

My friend Walt says if you look for something, you'll find it. He finds feathers. Everywhere. All the time. Now I find feathers as if I'm tuned into his cosmic call out! I tend to be more a heart person, but with a twist, complements of mother nature. I see heart-shaped leaves in all kinds of places—on the street, the beach, driveway, or parking lot. For some reason, my heart spirit animal appears in the form of a leaf.

I've now recruited my oldest child into this random act of heartness sightings, sending cell phone pics of heart-shaped leaves. Now I can't see one without thinking about Grif. And signs of love that appear when we name them. Such joy can be found in telling the universe we're open to find what's out there.

SET YOUR TABLE
Anything calling out to you that is waiting to be found?

The Unexpected Gift of Passion

My friend Pat gave my children the best gifts ever. Her presents had one requirement from the fortunate recipients—their passion. Both presents were unexpected, and the outcome has been, too.

Her first gift came during a rare lunch together. We live in different cities, and I had traveled to attend a meeting near her home. We met for a quick bite and caught up on life, which, inevitably, led to our children. Her two sons were grown and doing well. Her oldest was working on his graduate degree, yet still nurturing his love of music. I remember when he was younger and our families went to a Pat Metheny concert. I enjoyed watching her son, eyes wide toward the stage, as much as the famous jazz guitarist.

Her son is now a successful college educator who has become a proficient guitarist and married a talented musician he met in college.

As I got up to leave from lunch, my friend handed me a card for Griffin, who had recently turned 16. We didn't normally exchange gifts for our children, but this one was sentimental. Sixteen years prior, she drove a very pregnant me in premature labor from a meeting to a hospital 40 miles away.

Griffin opened the card that night after my lunch. "Oh wow. Mom, look at this." It was a very generous check. My friend and her husband wrote a note of what music had meant to their son. They knew Griffin had a guitar and asked only one thing: use their check toward guitar lessons.

So granted.

We met with our friends for lunch a year later. Grif played his guitar as we stood on the sidewalk outside the restaurant. It is one of those tender moments that will forever be locked in time for me.

Fast forward two years later. My daughter, Gillian, was turning 16. We were heading to an out-of-town high school volleyball tournament before her birthday. Before we left, a box addressed to Gilly arrived in the mail. She found a card inside from my friend and her husband along with a professional-grade digital camera.

My friend's husband discovered photography in his 50s. He has photographed his life, especially his international travels, in spectacular visual art. Like their gift to Griffin, this kind couple asked only one thing of Gilly in return: explore what the camera can do.

And boy has she. Well, actually, I did first.

I quickly learned the beauty of fast shutter speed to capture Gilly and her team winning their first high school state championship. And Gilly has used her lens to focus on extraordinary moments and people ever since, creating a blog photographing other epileptics who are thriving in spite of their condition.

Griffin is a young adult now. I'm a bit biased, but , gosh, talk about a terrific guitarist—a fan of all kinds of music, taking courses about musicians such as Django Reinhardt and John Coltrane.

Gilly just finished graduate school and parlayed her photography passion and a really good camera with a blog celebrating epileptics which led to a career in health care.

My children's lives have been enriched because someone made it possible for them to tap into the wellspring of passion. And this passion was fostered during a time when I could barely afford paying for groceries, let alone a music lesson or nice camera. Not that my friend knew this.

Nor could she imagine the emotional power of a jazz chordal progression heard from a nearby room or an inspirational blog written in Mexico.

Thank you, my friend.

SET YOUR TABLE

Give a passion gift to a young person. Both of your lives will be enriched.

A MOMENT WITH
Jose Juarez

I've known Jose for many years as he is married to my best friend, Kelly. It's been a joy to watch them grow into successful entrepreneurs who give generously to their community through love and food.

Q. Tell me about your journey to becoming ABC TV's "Live with Kelly and Michael's America's New Grill Star."
Jose: After seeing a promotion for the contest, I submitted a video sharing why I should be America's next grill star. I received a call letting me know I

was chosen as a semi-finalist. They flew my wife, Kelly, and me to New York City to close the show, grilling my BarbaCuban sandwich with Kelly Ripa and Michael Strahan. They narrowed it down to two finalists. We were judged by three Food Network stars who named me the winner.

Q. Who inspires you with your culinary creations?

Jose: I take most of my inspiration from my love of American BBQ and Cuban food. I was born in Cuba before fleeing with my family to the United States following Castro's Communist rule. My cooking is a reflection of my love for both countries.

Q. What led you to establish your popular sauce company?

Jose: After winning the national contest, many people wondered if we would start a restaurant and wanted to try our sauce. I had no interest in a running a restaurant, however, I had made sauces for many years. After great reviews, there was a demand for my 455 Sauce, so we entered the sauce world and

started the BarbaCuban Sauce Company in 2016. Now, we offer six additional sauces and our 455 Sauce is in Publix stores across Florida.

Q. Please share your favorite recipe.
Jose: Mojo Cuban Pulled Pork. This is so easy and good. Start with a 4-pound Boston butt. Place it in a deep pan. Pour one 12 oz. bottle of my BarbaCuban Mojo in the pan and cover with aluminum foil. Preheat oven to 325°F. Cook for 3 hours and reduce heat to 225°F. Cook for another two hours. Remove from pan and pull the pork. Save the juice to pour over the pork and rice.

Savoring Shermans on Doris Drive

I was driving my daughter and 90-year-old mother after lunch when I realized I had fallen short as a parent. Mom pointed to a concrete-block house. "That's the last house Sherman built before he retired," she said.

It was? Well, not exactly, but that's okay. Living on this planet for eight decades grants grace in memory.

It was, however, a home built by my late father. That's when it hit me: In my 20 years of raising children, I had neglected to show them an important piece of their grandfather's legacy.

Dad was a builder here in Ocala, building residential and commercial structures for most of his adult life. He built a lot of houses. I know. I lived in most of them. When your parent is a builder, you acquire the skill of adaptability. That's a nice way of saying when the spec house does not sell, the builder's family moves in.

Dad had a fondness for tri-level design and unique ones at that. Think Brady Bunch home meets Frank Lloyd Wright, sort of. As a kid, I loved it. I often had a new bedroom and, in fitting tri-level form, sometimes it was upstairs or on the bottom or main floor. Dad mixed it up each time.

In some ways, his work was a pace different than the others in the neighborhood. A Yeary home stood out in between the traditional Colonial brick and stucco houses. This didn't stop Dad from pushing the architectural envelope outside or in. My bedroom once had a built-in sitting area encased in mustard-yellow shag carpet floor to wall, a la Austin Powers.

Thinking of that bedroom adds to my maternal guilt.

Not too long ago, I found myself in that very neighborhood of my past, dotted with Sherman Yeary creations. I had not been there in years, but I took the long way home. Dad's houses lined the streets just off a main road once known as Doris Drive. I was a newborn on that street in a tri-level home not built by my father, which somehow doesn't seem right. But he made up for it with several houses immediately following it.

A flood of sentiment washed over me as I drove down the street where dad built three houses in a row. We lived in the middle one. Instantly, I was a pre-teen again lounging with my girlfriends in my shagged sitting nook on the second floor. I "helped" dad build the house to our left, walking a few steps out our front door to the work site with my makeshift toolbox he made just for me. I plastered my first drywall in that house.

To our right was a one-story spec that a mother and daughter bought from dad. They invited me over most Friday nights to eat s'mores made in their counter-top broiler. Driving by, I could taste melted chocolate on toasted marshmallow.

My sister lived two blocks away in a custom Yeary home where I'd walk most afternoons to babysit my young nieces. Dad liked to include big kitchens with living areas. He was always ahead of the design curve. I could make snacks and keep an eye on two active little girls.

Writer Pat Conroy opens his southern classic "Prince of Tides" writing, "My wound is geography." We would eventually move to other neighborhoods across town. An unsold spec house was calling.

For me, here—on old Doris Drive—geography was my salve. It was my sense of place grounding me with a builder's hand in familiarity and love.

I believe a family field trip is in order soon.

SET YOUR TABLE

Don't wait until it's too late. Take a drive down memory lane, literally, with friends and family. Show them places that shaped you.

Living Room

When I need to turn down the volume of life, I head to my living room. The only central gathering spot in our cozy abode, it serves as the hub for Mike and me since we are empty nesters. When we moved in, I bathed the room in neutral colors of cream and ivory with a splash of teal décor with wallpaper, pillows and accent furniture. Morning is my favorite time here when the sun washes everything in bright rays of gold. Absolute serenity.

SET YOUR TABLE

Bright color is fine, yet, try to carve a space that whispers instead of shouts. Your blood pressure will thank you.

The Chair

A détente has occurred in the elevated armchair hostilities. Mike and I have reached a truce that promises peace in our time, or, at least after dinner. We've agreed to share the coveted armchair by the front window that has been a sore spot ever since we moved into our current home.

What's so special about this chair? As realtors say, location, location, location. The teal and tan leopard upholstered seat with rolled arms is positioned in the corner for optimal viewing of our Smart TV. It also faces away from the front door toward the main living area and kitchen. And when the sun filters through the nearby window, you are wrapped in a warm blanket of coziness.

Thus, the marital strife—we both want *that* chair. I once gave seating rights for a whole week to Mike as part of his birthday gift. He was brought to tears. For Mother's Day, he reserved it for me. This is what quarantining during a pandemic has done to us, I think. We've gone mad.

Oh, I forgot to mention something—we own the *exact same chair* right next to our point of contention. I bought them as a pair with an antique oak side table in between. Yet, we fight over just the one. As in the one less than 20 inches away. This neglected seat never had a chance. Positioned next to the front door and away from the TV, the chair's comfort karma is missing.

Finally, we decided to alternate days and nights for supreme seating ownership. If I get the chair in the morning, it's Mike's at night. When Mike claims it for an afternoon to watch football, I'm the victor at cocktail hour.

I feel good about our armchair armistice. We've come a long a way to ease strained relations. Now we can focus on each other. And the ottoman on which we've both laid stake. Someone call the U.N. This one's gonna get dicey.

SET YOUR TABLE

Take time to nurture your relationship with someone special. Just don't take his or her chair.

June

Centerpieces: Revel

Summer gives permission to throw out schedules, put on the flip flops, and revel in sun-kissed afternoons. Even on the hottest days in Florida, the outside calls my name. So do low-country boils, spontaneous gatherings, white hydrangeas, Astrud Gilberto, mojitos, East Coast Swing Dancing, beach trips, beach walks, really, beach anything! This is the time when I throw caution and my checklist to the summer breeze and take in whatever feels right.

SET YOUR TABLE

Delight in the moment! Invite friends over for a summer cocktail and crank up your favorite summer tunes.

Little Miss Something

I'm living proof that mail-in contests are legitimate—sort of. When I was 10, my mother mailed a Polaroid photo of me to the Little Miss United States Pageant. For a minimal registration fee and willingness to pay all contest expenses to Lynchburg, Va., the apparent epicenter of Little Miss pageants,

I could be a contender. Four weeks later, Mom pulled a letter out of the mailbox and squealed all the way back to the house. Her baby girl was Little Miss Florida.

Just like that.

But Mom's vicarious dreams for a future Phyllis George were dashed at the Virginia state line. I was no match for the other contestants. These girls were professionals.

Miss Mississippi wore makeup and a big hoop skirt custom designed in New York City. Mom sewed my evening wear of white cotton fabric left over from an Easter tablecloth, adding sequined strawberry appliqués to the gown. I thought citrus was the official Florida fruit, but didn't want to upset Mom who was busy hot-gluing a strawberry to my hair barrette.

It was no surprise that Miss Mississippi won the coveted crown. I placed fourth runner-up and got a $100 savings bond. But Mama was happy. Her baby girl was fourth in the nation!

I swore off pageants until Kelly, my best friend in high school, entered us both in the Miss God and Country Day pageant, the Fourth of July contest sponsored by the Ocala Jaycees. Her boss at a local jewelry store was the pageant coordinator and badly in need of contestants. Kelly felt pressured to help. I wasn't so sure.

Amy Mangan

The day of the pageant arrived. Parading on stage in front of familiar faces in a bathing suit at the Ocala City Auditorium hadn't been on my list of things to do that summer. Even worse, each of us had to answer a current events question because all serious beauty pageants require contestants to be articulate about God, country, and nuclear proliferation while wearing a smokin' hot one-piece. Mom, still pining for her daughter's elusive crown, had found a silky, brown swimsuit on sale that was two sizes too big for me, especially, er, up top. She said brown was a winning color.

I looked like a big, flat Hershey's bar.

Kelly was more stylish, though shaking like a leaf. She asked to borrow my lip gloss. I was about to go on stage, so I told her to grab it from my purse.

That's when it happened.

A shrill came from behind the curtains. The other contestants and I ran to Kelly who was crying. She had mistakenly grabbed my black liquid eye liner, not the gloss. She tried furiously to rub it off, instead smearing it all over her face, looking like Alice Cooper in a swimsuit. The emcee pulled us both on stage. I'm not sure anyone heard Kelly's thoughtful answer about the economy. It's not every day you see a young woman in a bathing suit with a five o'clock shadow. Kelly handled the situation like a pro, looking straight ahead at the audience—smeared chin up—with nary a word of how Maybelline should more clearly label its beauty products.

Maybe it was pity for Kelly or sympathy for my ill-fitting swimsuit. Kelly and I came in first-runner-up and winner, respectively. The newspaper photo that ran the next day captured the incredulous look on both of our faces. But the real look of amazement was that of my mother's. Her baby girl had come a very long way from Lynchburg.

Just like that.

SET YOUR TABLE

Never make a dress out of a table skirt. However, if you do, wear it like you own it!

The Kitchen

Some days I walk around my white quartz-wrapped kitchen island and can't believe it is actually mine. Call it a scarcity mindset of past hard times, I'm forever grateful to be here. We purchased the house from friends—Chuck and MaryAnne—who had lovingly flipped it with tasteful décor touches like twin French chandeliers in the kitchen. Every wall was already painted in my color of choice, Sherwin Williams' Revere Pewter. Kismet, I tell ya.

And talk about kitchen space—I've got it for days! It's like Chuck and MaryAnne looked into my wish list soul and granted me everything I wanted—

ample cabinets, glossy white subway tile, black raw granite countertops on the perimeter, a walk-in pantry, and a kitchen island oozing style all the way to the nearby front door. No wonder Mike and I spend so much time here. Inevitably, this is also where friends and family convene and, on occasion, dance when I turn on the tiny counter disco ball given to me as a housewarming gift by friends Gil and Gail.

SET YOUR TABLE

The kitchen is always the best place to start and end a party, so whip out the invite list whether intimate or bigger. Disco ball not optional. Mine is available on Amazon.

Scar of Florida

I went to my hairstylist and left with a homemade casserole.

A mutual friend of ours had lost her husband and I was going to see her after my hair appointment.

Ruthy, my hairstylist, stopped cutting my hair mid-clip, placed her scissors on the shelf, rushed into the back room and returned with a frozen Mexican casserole she had made for our friend. I left her salon with a fresh cut and a beef tortilla dish.

That's what a fellowship of friends, neighbors and strangers do when there is pain.

We come together and figure out a way to help. We feed. We network for resources. We clean the house. We organize fundraisers. Sometimes, we just show up and listen. Often, we try to figure out how to help for just that minute, hour or day. We do little things and big things to lessen the burden.

Our gestures can't erase the loss, but we hope they can ease the hurt.

Our community is hurting once again. We lost a former local high school football player and current college player who was in the prime of his life—so prime that he was days away from his debut at the NFL Pro Day try-outs.

I didn't know this young man, but I know those who loved him and his family. We have come together to acknowledge the grief that is so present you can taste its bitter residue.

The grief remains, but there is communal love to buffer it for a while. To paraphrase author and pastor William A. Ritter, who lost his son to suicide, some pain cannot be explained, but it can be embraced.

So we embrace.

Several years ago, I visited a friend who is terminally ill. He was a respected and longtime local leader who made our home better in his quiet, determined way. I always considered him to be our consummate statesman, though he never ran for office. He didn't seek the political spotlight. He just wanted to make life better for those around him.

And he did. I was surprised when I walked into his room and saw two older men standing by his bed. They, too, had a hand at shaping our city and county into a thriving place to live. They were sharing stories about our friend. We talked about what he meant to each of us and to our community. We took turns holding his hand while remembering his leadership and kindness.

Author Anna Quindlen and her brother lost their mother and his wife at a young age.

"When does it stop hurting? We would have to answer in all honest candor: 'If it ever does, we'll let you know.'"

Grief leaves a permanent mark. Compassion leaves a space for love.

I've had opportunities to leave home and move away, and I did so a few times. But I kept coming back.

Once, I burned my hand in the kitchen, and it left a wrinkled, reddened blister that oddly resembled the shape of our state. I used to joke it was the "scar of Florida" serving as a visible reminder I can't leave this place. Over time, the mark faded, but this state, this town, this community—my community—is permanently etched in a sacred spot in my heart.

Where else can you get a haircut and casserole at the same place?

If you live here, this makes complete sense.

SET YOUR TABLE

Be a witness to others' grief who simply want you to reside in their space for a while.

A Treasure with Genuine Class

A local history buff called to tell me about two Ocala High School graduation rings that had been found.

One is from 1935, the other 1936, inscribed with the initials *BR* and *SFB* respectively. The 1935 ring was spotted on the sandy shores of Lake Weir, where, more than 80 years ago, the beach would have been the lake, making this discovery all the more remarkable. My friend assumed a private investigator role to deliver the rings to the owners or, most likely, their families.

This got me thinking about my high school class ring that I never owned. I had my sights on something else, a jewel found only at the finest (and only) catalog showroom in Ocala—Service Merchandise. It was a gold ring with a cluster of three opals. I visited the store's jewelry counter so often the sales clerk finally asked me if I had any intention of purchasing the ring.

My parents offered to buy me the official high school class ring, a kind offer knowing money was tight for my family as we were just peeling off the edge of our country's economic recession in the early '80s. Neither mom nor dad had the opportunity to go to college. They were proud their youngest daughter would soon graduate high school and attend college on scholarship.

The class ring was expensive, and I couldn't justify the cost for something I wasn't in love with.

But that opal ring, well …

It would be my first real piece of jewelry with precious gems and gold unlike the metal mood ring that colored my finger a moldy green. Plus, it was way cheaper than the class ring.

And it was kind of like the opal ring a girl in my class got for her 16th birthday a year prior, one I had since admired. In science class, she sat across the aisle from me and would hand me notes to pass to her best friend sitting behind me. When she'd hand me her note, her ring sparkled a faint light of envy in my eyes.

A few months before graduation, mom and dad surprised me at dinner with a gift bag from Service Merchandise placed on my dining table chair.

Sweet Jewels! My very own opal ring. The three gem-cluster was comprised of little opal-ish chips, probably lab-created in China. But I had my very own ring! Instructions for "Opal Care" were included in my gift bag, advising me to rub the stones in baby oil to prevent cracking. Every morning before school, I'd saturate my ring in oil so it would be protected and shiny the whole day through. And shiny it was. On my hands. On my clothes. The car steering wheel. My homework. Miss Social's notes that I passed to her BFF. (Hey, smudges happen.)

I wore the ring every day the rest of high school. And college. And graduate school.

But, somewhere between grad school and my first apartment, I lost my ring. Maybe it's buried in the sand somewhere waiting to be found. Unlike the Ocala High School rings, it does not bear engraved initials of its owner. But its meaning is forever etched in my heart, just not for the desires of an impressionable 17-year-old girl with oily hands.

When I think of my ring, I see my mom and dad at the dinner table beaming with wide grins. They didn't have to buy me a piece of jewelry. But they wanted to commemorate my rite of passage—high school graduation—with something I'd always remember.

And what I remember, what I cherish still to this day, was the memory of my parents centering their lives around their family, honoring celebrations big and small.

"What's that on your chair, honey?" my parents asked in feigned curiosity as I walked into the dining room.

Love. In a bag with instructions to care for that which is precious.

SET YOUR TABLE

Diamonds and opals are always your best friend. Shopping trip, anyone?

Café Lights

Bulb by bulb, my outdoor café lights are automatic mood enhancers. With the flip of a switch, my backyard becomes an illuminated vista of possibility. Beneath the garland of lights, I added a long table with benches that has become my favorite place to entertain. Sometimes, I like to stand on my back porch and take in the view before joining the others at the table—white lights, good friends, more food than anyone can consume (I *am* my mother, after all), Chet Baker on the weatherproof portable speaker, the clinking of wine glasses, laughter.

Love by luminescence? I'll take it!

SET YOUR TABLE

It's amazing what a few strands of light can do for a space and spirit. Go forth and get thee some!

Powerball Dreaming

I become a serious gambler—scratch off tickets—during the summer because I must have that St. Augustine house!

The Powerball lottery frenzy visited my family. My husband bought some tickets and left them on the kitchen counter until the winning numbers were announced. We never play, but the cash payout was close to a gazillion dollars and, well, gazillion piqued our interest. Our chances of winning were significantly less than getting struck by lightning or One Direction reuniting. It was the "Hunger Games" of statistical reality—the odds were not in our favor.

Consequently, we did not speak of our irrational purchase until the day after the drawing. That's when the fun began.

I made a cup of coffee while Mike checked the morning newspaper for the Powerball winning numbers. Holding the tickets in his hand, he copiously scanned the paper like an IRS auditor. I stayed in the adjoining kitchen, hesitant to ask the outcome. Did we win gazillions or lose a few bucks on some Quick Picks? Either way, I'd need caffeine.

Mike looked up. "Well, we're not multi-millionaires. Let's not quit our jobs," he said with a half-smile. I grabbed his favorite coffee mug, the ceramic one with cute dog paintings that the children gave him years ago.

He'd need some strong java.

I sat next to him and grabbed a section of the paper. We read in silence for a few minutes.

"You know what I'd do if I'd have won?" I said with my reading glasses perched on my nose.

And for the next half hour, we shared our spending fantasies. Some were big, others small. But here's what surprised me—or, once I thought about it, didn't surprise me at all. We shared the exact same dreams, especially our first investment of choice.

First thing we'd do after providing for our family? Donate to our doctors to advance research in the fields of diabetes and epilepsy. And in a really big way that would make an impact. We'd give enough to help patients and their families better manage their lives. Then we'd give our college-aged children money to contribute to causes that matter to them. Next? Bus stop covers for our community so no one has to wait for a ride in bad weather without shelter.

And on we went, getting more excited by our grand plans. After a few minutes, it dawned on us that we didn't talk about the obvious purchases one would typically make—buy a home, car, large TV with one flippin' remote instead of five. The obvious things. Stuff, really. When you get to our age, you are so over the stuff. You're about the substance. And we both agreed that neither one of us would quit our jobs if we'd have won the lottery. We love what we do and are lucky as all get out to work with great teams. Why quit?

So what if we can't endow a center that will cure diabetes and epilepsy? Or cover the county with bus stop shelters? We can still advocate for these causes. And raise money. And volunteer. That much, we can do.

As we sat on our couch sipping our coffee talking about what we didn't win, we realized what we had right in front of us.

That morning, I woke up and hopped out of bed and put on my favorite nubby socks. I poured myself a strong cup of coffee. I did not wake up a gazillionaire.

But, I woke up.

And I woke up happy.

What are the chances I can make a difference for causes in which I believe and those whom I love? I'd like to think they are pretty good.

May those odds ever be in my favor.

SET YOUR TABLE

Make your own lottery ticket, but one full of intangible wins you may already have. If not, create them.

A MOMENT WITH
Karley Holland

An aspiring interior designer and architect while still in high school, Karley has started her incredible journey of creating beautiful spaces.

Q: What inspired you to follow this passion?

Karley: When I first discovered the amazing app of Pinterest, I knew right then and there that I wanted to be an interior designer and architect. Photos of houses appeared on my "browse page" and I immediately fell in love. I created multiple folders and started designing my dream home! With this new sudden interest, my dad and I would drive around before school looking at houses.

My family allowed me the freedom to decorate the seasonal porch. I helped pick out and plant the flowers for spring and summer, the pumpkins and hay bales for autumn and the small Christmas trees for winter.

For my birthday, I asked my mom if I could redo my room. We went to Homegoods and I was allowed to pick out everything for my new room! I decided to paint the walls a light blue and chose an accent wall of navy. I had various textured and sized pillows on my bed and put faux flowers from Hobby Lobby on the frame of a floor mirror. This was my first project, not necessarily my best! However, I am very grateful that I was able to have this opportunity. It allowed me to grow as a designer and a person as I had to make decisions and be practical about them.

Q: Do you have a signature look and color preference?

Karley: When designing a space, my go-to look is definitely modern coastal. I love to incorporate blues and whites in a space as, in my opinion, they bring a sense of serenity. Designs inspired by water make me feel comfortable and welcomed.

@lifeonlkn

"I aspire to make spaces for people... that they can call their own."

My favorite design brand is Serena and Lily. They provide sophisticated and elegant furniture with a slight coastal twist. With the right sales and promotion codes, I like to encompass their pieces within our home. This company has reached out to me on social media asking if they could include my designs in their portfolio. One of my favorite pieces of theirs is hands down the Riviera Counter Stool that I have included in some of my clients' kitchens.

Within my designs, I like incorporating rattans, grasscloths, jutes, sisals, and other materials of varying texture. I also admire the current trend of bringing wallpaper back. It is such a powerful design element as it can transform a room from being mediocre to thrilling, exciting, and spontaneous.

Styling built-in bookcases is one of my most favorite things to do. They can always be rearranged and constantly changed. While making them look amazing with various decorative accessories is fun, they also in a way represent the family living within the home. These shelves display family photos, memorabilia, and achievements, creating a touching moment to the viewer.

Q: Who are your designer role models?
Karley: Designers and architects who inspire me are Amanda Orr, The Fox Group, Bria Hammel, Shea McGee, and Megan Molten. I admire how each of their personal styles are different, however when viewing their portfolio, they have curated a range of different styles and designs to accommodate their clients and their needs. They are all located in different parts of the country, which is very intriguing to see how geographic location influences design. I have learned so much from these designers and architects regarding this field and look forward to and anticipate learning more!

Q: What are your future plans?
Karley: While I still have much to learn, my future plans are to someday own an architect and interior design firm. It would be my dream to help a client throughout the homebuilding and designing process. Guiding them from designing their home's floor plan to picking out the fabric of the pillows on their sofa. I would be able to design a home plan with furnishings and accessories in mind, striving to make it a true piece of art that is tailored to the client's style and functionality needs. I aspire to make spaces for people so that when they pull into their driveway they are excited to relax and enter a beautiful home that they can call their own.

Meeting a Legend

Within five minutes of meeting John, he gave me a Johnny Matanzas and the Hombres CD, played a bluesy tune on the harmonica, then, deftly explained Florida's Gulf Coast ecosystem restoration post-Deepwater Horizon. By all accounts, this was classic John Hankinson, a larger-than-life personality and esteemed environmentalist. We met at an Audubon Florida assembly with the promise to meet again to discuss water issues.

"Come to our beach house and bring your family, too," John added after hearing my son played guitar. "We can play a few songs in my studio."

"I sure will," I said, waving goodbye across the hotel conference room.

This was the first and last time I met the famous John Henry Hankinson, Jr.

Soon after, John passed away due to complications from a brain hemorrhage. He was 68.

Across the country, tributes to John started pouring in as news of his death was made public. Online and printed accolades shared universal praise of a hands-on leader who took complex environmental challenges seriously, but himself, not so much. When he led the EPA's Region 4 office in Atlanta, he formed a blues-rock band with some of his co-workers, The Nonessentials, as government shutdowns deemed many in his agency as "nonessential." John balked at the notion and advocated for his team.

John never shied away from working on difficult projects and encouraged others to join him with one requirement—to literally go where the problem was, be it a polluted swampland or a toxic coast. No executive office quarterbacking for John. He believed the only way to fix a problem was to experience it.

After John's death, I stayed up late one night reading story after story about the man many called "Big Puff." It's rare to smile and tear up at the same time when reading a memorial, but, then again, John was pretty exceptional.

He was a lawyer, musician, environmental defender, policy leader, and, apparently, a heck of a barbecue chef.

He was also a dedicated father, husband, son and brother, hailing from an Ocala family whose mother, father, sisters and brother could each merit a column of their own for their noteworthy contributions to our world. Matter of fact, that's how I came to know of John, through his sister, Margaret Hankinson Spontak, a well-regarded leadership strategist and environmental author in her own right.

"You've got to meet my brother, John," Margaret would often say to me, knowing our mutual interests.

Time passed. I let life get in the way of making an opportunity to meet John who lived just two hours away near the Matanzas Inlet, hence the inspiration for his latest band and CD. I even re-scheduled a few introductory phone calls for some reason I can't recall.

It was by chance that we actually met, both of us sitting next to each other at the same table for Audubon's opening session luncheon. He was on the agenda to speak about the Gulf Coast restoration. We hugged instantly, feeling like old friends thanks to one persistent sister.

"Margaret will be so happy we finally met," we both said almost in unison.

We took a cellphone selfie, texting it to Margaret, the friend-matchmaker.

"Won't she get a kick that her brother is in a selfie?" John laughed as we leaned in to pose for the picture.

Then, he pulled out something from his worn-leather briefcase.

"Here's something you and your son may enjoy," John said, handing me a CD titled "Holding Down the Fort" by Johnny Matanzas and the Hombres, a nod to vigilant protection of our Florida history and ecosystem near Fort Matanzas.

After John's eloquent and passionate presentation on the precarious state of our gulf which ended with a spontaneous harmonica solo that rose the sold-out crowd to a standing ovation, we said our goodbyes with assurance we'd see each other again.

I popped his CD in my car laughing and singing all the way back from St. Pete to Ocala. From the starting track of "Who is that Hombre?" to "Maggie's Farm," I knew I was listening to something special.

That was five months ago.

Confession: I'm not a rock-blues kind of girl, but this CD hasn't left my car. I have a favorite: "I Ain't Old (Been Around a Long Time)" by Delbert McClinton, sung by John who crooned as if he was singing his way to conviction about living a life without regret.

The CD stays in my play track.

As does the one and only larger-than-life John Hankinson.

I'm grateful my procrastination didn't keep me from meeting John Hankinson. He made time for what and who mattered to him, from music to the marshes. And I know how lucky I am that time made it briefly possible for me to meet a legend.

Take a look around you. Chances are John's legacy is preserved in the air you breathe, the water you drink, and land you love.

You're right, Margaret. I'm awfully glad I met your brother.

SET YOUR TABLE

Seek out the formidable heroes and tell them what they mean to you.

July

Centerpieces: Protect

After Mama died, my sisters and I decided to attempt a multi-family reunion at our favorite place, Crescent Beach. No small feat since we were spread out from Georgia to California, yet, we prevailed and landed side-by-side-by-side-by-side oceanfront condos where we had spent many a summer vacation. We had nieces, nephews by love, babies, cousins, more babies, aunties—as beloved nieces like to call my sisters and me—and dear friends who are like family.

For me, the best part of each day was after dinner in my condo since I was on the first floor, easy steps for the restless little ones to venture onto the patio. Matt is married to my niece Lisa and is not only an exceptional cook—Thomas Keller is his chef hero if that tells you anything—but also a pastor. Translation: he knows how to herd a crowd. Matt corralled us into a circle.

Then we counted off trying to remember our respective number. The rules go like this—you clap twice, slap your thigh twice, then yell a number. Said number repeats the pattern and shouts another number. If you dare to stumble, and many a poor soul does, you're out of the game. The goal is to be last person standing, er, slapping. Hunger Games Meets the Math Bee.

Off we went! We clapped, slapped twice and shouted numbers. Sister Cindy was automatically out. She did the epic Yeary cry/laugh caving in before she could even sputter a number. I found myself mentally sizing up the competition. Who else would fall so easily? Yell their number. But, first, I had to remember my own. Damn. This game is harrrrrd. After a few rounds, we called a truce. The young folk—aka those with nimble brain cells—prevailed.

It's summer again. While I recognize the difficulties in coordinating multiple families' calendars, oh, how I hope we return to the beach. And that I'll remember my number.

Which is exactly what Mama would want.

SET YOUR TABLE

Don't wait for a family reunion. Make the effort. It's worth it.

The Reading Worm

Summer evokes pleasure, be it a vacation, lighter work load, or, in my case, more time for reading.

During my adolescent years when pop-star David Cassidy held me in rapt attention, my father provided a wonderful discursion on Sunday afternoons as we read our favorite book of the moment together.

This love of the printed word followed me to middle school when my homeroom teacher held a reading worm contest. Each student's name was placed on a construction paper circle. Upon completion of reading a book, the title was added to a circle next to the student's name. The rules were simple. The student with the longest worm at the end of the month won.

I got busy reading and quickly, my circles started adding up although I had competition. A young man in class announced he would win the contest as he won every other academic competition in school. His goal in life was to be the President of the United States. Dressing for success, he carried a black leather briefcase to school. Soon, we were neck and neck, or should I say, worm and worm.

The final week approached—we were down to our last book. I chose Jonathan Livingston Seagull. Mr. President chose Charlie and The Chocolate Factory. I was hoping he would have chosen something more difficult like Oliver Wendell Holmes's abridged version of legal opinions. He'd know this fictional work backways and sideways and underways. Great. Now I was talking like Willie Wonka.

Our teacher announced we would give an oral presentation of our final selection. Mr. President volunteered to go first, a classic political strategy to unnerve one's opponent. He sailed through, making it look so easy, like Kennedy in the Nixon-Kennedy debates.

I felt like Nixon, weak, pale, and confused. Panic overtook me and I couldn't remember who Jonathan was. He had wings. Yes, he had wings. He was a bird.

Okay, things were coming together. I was stalling. The class was staring. Mr. President was glaring while straightening his clip-on tie.

Closing my eyes tightly, I was back in my bedroom reading with Dad about a young and naïve seagull who believed he could do better. A bird punished for his personal choices, yet liberated above his peers by creating his own journey and inspiring others to do the same. Thinking about Jonathan comforted me. I was no intellectual match for Mr. President and that was okay. I could fly anyway. I'd take my own path even if it wasn't the road to the White House.

Silence. Then the teacher muttered something about my thoughtful analysis.

What analysis? Was I thinking out loud? Did I call my competitor "Mr. President?" The teacher announced I won the contest, a first for me. In disbelief, I thanked everyone saying winning didn't matter. Who was I kidding? I beat the future leader of the free world! Yet, glory is a fleeting prize as the teacher told us to return to our seats and open our math books.

Mr. President went on to realize many accomplishments, including graduation from Harvard. He's not President…yet, but is a successful lawyer in the Midwest. In the meantime, it's a beautiful day in Ocala as we've begun the Third Annual Mangan Family Reading Worm Contest with multicolored circles spread across the kitchen's bulletin board. My oldest is leading by a worm after completing the Chronicles of Narnia, but Gillian just checked out Little Women and can't put it down. Better watch out. This has the makings of a terrific summer.

SET YOUR TABLE

Reading Worm Contests are always a good idea, regardless of age. Get reading! Construction paper worms, optional.

I ♥ My Friends

Few vacations result with a customized poem, but when I'm with our Movie Club, anything is possible. Mike and I enjoyed a trip to Asheville to be reunited with our beloved friends after a pandemic-induced far-too-long break. We celebrated our 21-year friendship, which began with watching movies and has since evolved into an unbreakable bond of love, respect, laughter, support, and trips together. At one point, we all lived within walking distance from each other on the same street before Chick and Sara and Hellen and Walt moved to different cities and states.

While exploring downtown Asheville, we discovered Carey who creates poems on the spot. He asked us to share a few key words about our special group and, twenty minutes later, he presented us with this beautiful keepsake.

Later in the week, we enjoyed lunch on the veranda of the historic Grove Park Inn where my friends surprised me with six hearts for the "Hearts" section of my recently published book, *Accent Pieces*, where I penned an essay about them. Then, they pulled out copies of my book and toasted our friendship story with champagne!

Six of them, six hearts for me, now all lovingly placed in new pottery purchased on the trip, keepsakes I will forever cherish.

SET YOUR TABLE
What symbolizes your bond with friends?

Serenading the Summer of Mary Kay

Memorable summer vacations hold their own special lore—the beach vacations of sand, sun and too-close sharks, camp nights sneaking into the cafeteria after curfew (I was a hungry child) and tubing down Ichetucknee's ice cold springs are a few of mine. Yet, my most iconic summer trip was the time I rode 1,000 miles to meet Mary Kay and rode back with Barbra Streisand.

I owe this memory to Mama, who loved Mary Kay Ash, the larger-than-life Texan cosmetic entrepreneur, almost as much as her husband and four daughters. Maybe out of necessity with a house full of women, Mama became a Mary Kay "beauty consultant" in the early 1970s. She converted our kitchen pantry into a make-up inventory closet lined with shelves of Mrs. Kay's iconic bubble-gum pink products.

When it came to direct sales, Mama was a natural. She held make-up parties around our dining room table and recruited other eager women to join the sales force. Soon she was top of the distribution team in Central Florida, earning her an invitation to meet Mary Kay herself at the annual cosmetic convention in Dallas. She could barely contain herself. She was about to meet her hero.

Except for one minor detail.

Money was tight, our family car—a high-mileaged Oldsmobile—had a temperamental relationship with its air conditioning system and we only had enough money to budget for a quick trip from Florida to Texas. Daddy did the math, put his five girls in the old Olds and got behind the steering wheel.

"We can do this, and it's gonna be a long drive," he said determinedly. "But, I brought something for the ride."

He held up two new eight-track tapes, one of comedian Jerry Clower, the other the "Hello Dolly" movie soundtrack with Walter Matthau and Barbra Streisand. By the time we hit the Texas state line, I knew Clower's "Coon Huntin'" routine by heart.

Our Dallas visit was brief, but long enough for Mama to meet Mary Kay, who was decked in all white from her hair to her white patent leather shoes, making her candy-apple red lipstick stand out like an exclamation mark. She was stunning with a flawless, porcelain-like complexion. The extra emollient night cream had clearly paid off.

After taking a few photographs of mom with Queen Mary, we hopped back into the car and headed home. Mama was on Cloud Nine.

"Sherman, did you hear Mary Kay say how pretty our girls are?" Mama asked Daddy as the Dallas skyline blurred behind us. "She was so nice and just as purty as her picture in our sales brochures."

As a treat on the long drive back, Daddy put the "Hello Dolly" tape into the car stereo player. Dolly Levi, aka Barbra Streisand, sang us straight through to Louisiana before trouble began.

"Uh-oh," Daddy said scowling at the car dashboard, "The air isn't working."

"Oh, no, Daddy!" cried my older sisters whose bouffant hair would surely fall from the heat in spite of prolific use of hair spray. "We can't last in this car all the way back to Florida!"

"Roll the windows down and I'll get us home as soon as I can," he said staring straight ahead, probably wondering if he could survive being in an un-air-conditioned car with five women on the hottest day of summer.

When we reached Pensacola, the fiery temperature inside the car had warped the eight-track at the most inopportune time—Dolly Levi was just about to be serenaded with the signature "Hello, Dolly" number. Not to be distracted, Dad kept driving. The chorus sang as if they were underwater and in slow motion at the same time.

"Waaaaeeeeeellllll, Haaaaaaaalllllllooooooo, Daaaaaaawwwwwllly!";

My sisters, sweaty and tired, begged Daddy to turn off the tape.

"Come on, girls, sing it with me," he said with a big grin.

"Halllllooooo, Daaawwwwwwllly! Waaaeelll, haaaaallllooo dawllly!"

Being the youngest and most naïve to parental ways of distraction, I started singing. Then Donna joined. Then Cindy. Then Julie. They began laughing at the absurdity of it all, laughing so hard until they were crying.

And when we finally arrived home in the middle of a summer night, Mama was the last one singing with a smile as big as Mary Kay.

SET YOUR TABLE
Just for fun, listen to "Hello, Dolly."

Amid Any Storm, Try Not to Be a Label Maker

North Carolina's Outer Banks Motor Lodge posted a sign this week: "It's all fun and games until Jim Cantore shows up." Admittedly, I have the same visceral reaction about the weather warrior meteorologist. One look at him on the TV screen and I sense a hurricane headache coming on.

I kind of feel sorry for the guy. Who wants to be associated with fear and dread? This got me thinking about labels we connect to others. While weather reporters understand that grim perceptions sometimes occur as a result of their jobs, the rest of us may bear a similar fate if we're not careful.

You know the type—the person you see in the grocery store aisle that will corner you and rehash his personal everything-in-my-life-has-gone-wrong history for the next 30 minutes until the ice cream in your cart has melted. Or the neighbor who keeps a running list of grievances against fellow neighbors. The minute you see them, you've sized them up. Guilt by association, or, in many cases, historical evidence. So I've identified a few of these gloomy dispositions into what I'm unofficially calling *The Jim Cantore Personality Type*.

Type 1: The Worrier

For this person, the storm is always present. He lives in doubt and freely spreads his anguish to anyone close by. A worrier can't enjoy life's good tidings because he is convinced something bad is lurking just around the corner. If you congratulate him on an accomplishment, he'll give you a list of why his success will be short-lived. And he is more than happy to tell you why your successes will be brief and rare, too. He's the Debbie Downer who has a needle ready to burst an optimistic thought.

Type 2: The Alarmist

This storm is going to be the worst ever! And the one after that even worse! Consider this person as the Cassandra of friends and associates who make fear-mongering a competitive sport. It's hard to breathe around an Alarmist because she is sucking all the oxygen out of the doomed room. She's the co-worker who squelches collaboration on a project because it's going to be shot down by upper management. Or the friend who dismisses your dream to return to college as a fool's errand.

Type 3: The Impostor

The storm isn't what it seems for those who have a flair for the dramatic. Dare I submit The Weather Channel's Mark Seidel as evidence? Since reporting on a blustery street in Wilmington, North Carolina, he's taking a battering of public opinion for acting pummeled by high winds as two passersby strolled easily behind him, seemingly unaffected by the storm. It's hard to know where you stand with an Impostor because he shapeshifts more than a Harry Potter creature. He's prone to gossip, making mountains from molehills usually at the expense of someone else. And bigger is always better for an Impostor when passing along a scoop about someone else. But don't be surprised when you open Facebook the next day to see him gushing praise about that very same person.

In the spirit of ganging up on Jim Cantore, there's actually a Weather Channel commercial showing people fleeing from restaurants and beaches when Cantore appears. Make sure people don't flee from you because you've been tagged as a negative Nelly.

I mean no harm to Jim Cantore. I'm sure he's a nice guy. I just don't want to see him in my town anytime soon.

SET YOUR TABLE.
Fear not when facing a storm. It will pass.

A Word from a Digitized Elder

Dear young adults of the modern world and Snapchat,

Back in the day when people still used a phone book and shopped at malls instead of Amazon, your elders recorded events on a suitcase-sized video camera. The end product was a tape that we would watch once, label with a generic title no one would recall, then store it somewhere to collect dust. A great system.

Except for when everything went to compact discs.

So, we transferred our boxes of tapes onto CDs and watched them once more before packing them beside the family scrapbooks (those large leather binders your mothers pull out on birthdays). A great system.

Except for when everything went digital.

You see where this is going, right?

Which leads me to one of the best gifts I've given to myself: I shipped my CDs and videotapes to a company that returned them to me via email. Now I have decades of memories on my laptop and something called a "cloud" that I never update. And—get this—I can share these life jewels with one simple click. Voila! This experience has been so rewarding that I've become a digital-memory-sharing fool, texting and emailing recordings to friends and family whose response is usually, "Oh. My."

What? This has been around for a while, you say? Look, no one likes a smarty pants. Give a middle-aged woman a break.

My sisters were very impressed, OK? Yes, one of them still uses a phone book. And your point would be what, exactly?

A word of advice: At some point in your life, you will visit home. Your mom or dad or loved one over the age of 50 will invite you to sit on the couch for a minute. Hold on. Put down your iPhone. Your fake Instagram can wait. (See? I know things.) Take a deep breath as they turn on their laptop, click on a folder to another folder to a subfolder with a link that doesn't work. Keep breathing.

"Here it is!" your elder will exclaim as a video appears.

It's you in spectacular digitized glory appearing on the screen at your second birthday party when you wanted to play with the paper more than the present. When the celebration spotlight became just a tad too bright for your young, paper-loving soul and the screaming of your toddler birthday guests and Aunt Martha shoving cake in your mouth propelled you to fall into an emotional puddle in the middle of the kitchen floor. And when your mom, the resident crisis-mitigation expert, rushed to rescue you also accidentally knocked off the Curious George birthday cake which fell on top of her and you and Aunt Martha.

That video.

"Isn't this wonderful?" your elder will ask, wiping away a tear. "Let's watch your first bath next."

Here is what I want you to do, oh young one. Four simple suggestions:

1. Pause before saying a word. Then respond with "OK. I'd love to watch another video." Say it with conviction like you're watching Kendrick Lamar's new music video. Emote.
2. Don't point out that your parents wore the same outfit at every recorded event. They were exhausted. It's a miracle they got dressed, let alone managed life, kids and everything in between.
3. Laugh when the elder laughs.
4. Refrain from leaving the couch or checking your phone.

On this last point, I recommend soaking in the fact that you are sitting beside someone who loves you enough to want to do nothing more than be with you and watch home videos of you and relive special moments about you.

See? It's really all about you. It always has been. If you are lucky enough to figure this out, hug your weeping elder and make that moment about you both.

Then take a mental photograph. Trust me on this one, you'll be glad you did. Especially about 30 years from now when a young one comes to visit and you ask your robot to project a very special recording in a 3D hologram.

"See that?" you'll ask, wiping away a tear. "This was my second birthday and there are your grandparents. They loved you and me very much."

You're welcome.

Sincerely,
A Digitized Elder

SET YOUR TABLE

We elders are a sentimental lot. Indulge us. Watch old family tapes converted to holographs because by the time you read this, that will probably be the next big thing.

The Rhinestone Writer

No one can accuse me of being a fashion icon.

My favorite piece of clothing—a red velour sweatsuit—is deemed by my kids as my "Golden Girls" outfit. I still own a jacket with shoulder pads. And I'm certain, in time, the banana hair clip will come back in style.

While I'm not a candidate to offer fashion advice, I am empathetic to those who suffer the wrath of the style police. Maybe this has something to do with the unfortunate prom dress selection in high school, but I've totally put that behind me (she says, eye twitching.)

So, when the recent red carpet critiques hit the press, I got a little defensive.

Take Sophia Loren at the Oscars. Critics labeled her a "Tiered Terror" with her gold evening gown. Granted, I've seen better, but, the elegant Sophia makes 74-years-old look like the new 30.

Others slammed Beyonce's mermaid-styled dress and took jabs at her mother. Lighten up. She wore her mom's design! Besides, Queen Bey could wear a brown bag and look smokin' hot, so back off, Kanye.

It seems as though fashion has eclipsed everything.

Do we care more about what Meryl Streep wears than her brilliant acting career? And, correct me if I'm wrong, but history was made on a cold January day, and it wasn't that Michelle Obama wore green pumps.

Before I sound too high and mighty, I've succumbed to fads on occasion because a fashion magazine said I could reinvent my life simply by investing in an overpriced rhinestone belt. One day, I proudly wore my blinged accessory while teaching a college history class. Think American Revolution Meets Prada. Hello, world! Meet the new Prof. Amy! I'm reinvented!

One of my students walked up to the podium and said, "Nice belt, Mrs. Mangan. My grandma has one like that."

The belt looked great on Heidi Klum. On me, I looked like Hedda Hopper.

My longtime friend Kelly, who, as luck would have it, happens to be a fashion stylist, has reminded me through the years of the difference between style and trends. Style is finding a classic cut pair of slacks that makes you look and feel good. A trend is when you buy jeans with pleats. And you're short. Hellooooo, hips!

Style is sticking with colors that accentuate your features. A trend is buying a yellow sleeveless dress when both pale skin tone and flabby middle-aged arms beg for a better option.

Fashion designer Yves St. Laurent said, "Fashions fade, style is eternal."

How true. Style is a verb; fashion, a footnote. To me, style is the complete package. How a woman carries herself is more important than what a woman carries, regardless if it's a Chanel handbag.

I know women who exude style. They have the right combination of confidence, grace and humility… characteristics you can't find on a clothing rack.

Composure is the ultimate chic. It's better than any belt, but my velour sweatsuit is a keeper, kids.

Set your table Make your own kind of fashion. No one can rock velvet like you, dear.

SET YOUR TABLE
Add a little bling to your life today.

August

Centerpieces: Reflect

As summer fades into fall, this is the perfect time to measure expectations about the remaining year. For me, the months of October through December are a blur. Usually, I come up short managing the whirl of activities this season brings. By December 24th, I wonder what happened to all the months before when I promised to finish buying and wrapping gifts before Thanksgiving. Still, hope springs eternal as August bids goodbye, inviting me to tackle the calendar and shopping lists.

This is when I make a conscientious effort to reflect on what I hope January 1 looks like. Not skipping past the best parts of the season, mind you, but, rather, anticipating what I want to ensure is a priority from Halloween to New Year's Eve. Without fail, it's always the same goals from year to year, give or take a few:

- Be present in each moment
- Spend time with family and friends
- Done is better than perfect (this includes cooking a turkey)
- Make mindful purchases for gifts that reflect the receiver
- Add a new tradition or tweak an existing one
- Buy new Christmas stockings (This has been on my list for years)
- Don't overcommit or overeat

SET YOUR TABLE

Create your holiday intention list appreciating what level of satisfaction the season can bring.

Booking a Dream

Eons ago, in a crowded makeshift office in my storage closet, I wrote a novel. Every morning before work and most nights after the kiddos went to bed, I'd huddle next to stacks of totes and type. Looking back, I have no idea how I managed to dedicate energy to such an effort. I also had zero notion if my manuscript would ever see the light of publishing day. Yet, it didn't matter. A cast of characters kept dancing in my brain until I gave them life on paper. Best part? I loved every creative minute of the process.

Recently, I was talking to Bailey, my daughter's close friend who is also the editor of several of my books, this one included. Here's the thing about Bailey: not only is she a keen wordsmith, she also in possession of a high degree of emotional intelligence, a winning combo for a writer. Sometimes after we've reviewed a piece, our conversation turns to Bailey's own writing goals. She's got a book in her, she just knows it. I know it, too. I've seen her work and she's got what it takes. The only thing stopping Bailey is, well, Bailey. She rattled off the reasons preventing her from reaching this goal and it was clear to me she was suffering from an acute case of the "if onlys." We've all been there, lamenting what is possible if only other hurdles were removed.

If only I had more time.

If only I could quit my job to follow my passion.

If only it wasn't so hard to get published.

If only…

Here's the thing, I said—speaking as someone with the vantage point of experience, age, and a bit of wisdom—there will always be hurdles. There is never an ideal time to pursue a passion. Plus, the creative muse is a fickle one and won't hang around forever. I knew if I didn't commit to birthing my story, it would be gone. That was motivation enough.

I also shared another bit of advice my Dad often told me "Worry is crossing a bridge you may never reach." Forget about getting a publisher, I told her. Focus on clicking a few words together on the computer. Then do it again.

I'm no Oprah, but I've been there, done that walking down the path of unfulfilled dreams. And, I might add, unrealistic ones at that. Chances are my pithy words won't top a bestseller list or flicker on the big screen. Totally cool with this. Early on, I discovered I enjoy creating for those whom I love. I write for my family. I decorate and entertain for beloved friends. And I also find joy in satisfying one of the toughest customers of all—*me*. Sometimes, a turn of phrase or the Anthropologie pillows I found on sale just make me happy.

My birthday is in August. Over the course of a few years, I've published two books during this month—my memoir, *This Side Up,* and the novel written in a storage closet, *The History Lesson*. Even though the publisher selected the publication dates, I took this as a very good sign. This year, when it's time to blow out the candles, I'll make a wish…and then I'll make it happen.

SET YOUR TABLE

Time and dreams wait for no one, so what are you waiting for?

Go-To Friends

Do you have "go-to" friends who jump at a chance to help? That's Vanessa and Robyn for me. Here's what I love about them—I simply send a text with a message that usually goes like this, "I've got X to do, would you like to help?" Whatever X is, they're in! Organizing a home for a family with a sick child in the hospital, raising funds for others, and, as evident in this photo, assembling lots of promo packages for one of my book releases.

Even better, they make the process fun. We laughed, chatted, listened to Earth, Wind & Fire and drank a bit of wine while putting together flimsy cardboard boxes together that looked deceptively sturdy in my online shopping cart.

They make everything better, even uncooperative boxes.

SET YOUR TABLE

Who are your "go-to" friends? Let them know how much they mean to you.

Dad's Crowning Glory

I'm hooked on watching "Monarchy: The Royal Family at Work," the PBS series about the modern British monarchy. We're oddly drawn to the global fascination of the queen, a woman who reigns over, but does not govern, her country. After all this time, you'd think the world would have tired of the rather outdated concept of a royal family. Yet the PBS show boasts strong ratings.

My Anglican obsession comes naturally; my father was a bit of a royal fan, too. Dad was stationed with the Navy Air Corps in England during World War II.

As a young man who seldom ventured beyond the Marion County line, living in another country introduced new experiences. The war shaped dad for the rest of his life. So he spent the rest of his life preserving the indelible lessons of fighting for just causes, losing buddies too soon and living as if each day could be his last.

Something else stuck with dad—a culture he could not forget. A tradition he warmly embraced. History he vowed to remember. And food he would always crave. Dad should have bought stock in British shortbread cookies for all he purchased on return trips to England. He was a purist, too, as he swore the British shortbread sold in America wasn't authentic (this coming from the boy who grew up on Southern biscuits). But, he was a man who knew his flour.

Which is why I love telling the story of when dad met the queen.

My parents and I were visiting York, England with a friend of mine from college. Dad couldn't believe his luck when he read the newspaper that morning. The queen was to do a "walk about" in town—a fancy phrase for stating she would walk among the crowds to chat and collect flowers and act all royal. Dad checked his watch. If we hurried, we could find a primo spot to wait for, oh, another four hours until she arrived.

Grrrrreat.

So we waited. And waited.

I held a large sign dad made that read, "Your Florida Friends Say 'Hello!'"

The royal couple arrived. Prince Phillip commented on dad's sign asking what part of Florida he was from. When dad said, "Ocala," the prince smiled.

"I've ridden horses from Ocala!" said Prince Philip, who motioned to the queen as she walked toward dad.

"Ah, yes, lovely horses there," she said.

It was almost too much. Dad maintained composure although he forgot to introduce the rest of us to the royal couple. You couldn't see us behind our sign anyway. Dad was busy chatting with his new friends about the Florida equine industry he suddenly seemed to know a lot about.

Soon enough, the queen had to move on. She thanked dad for visiting. He thanked her for thanking him. Dad smiled for days after. Years, really.

Not bad for an American cousin with a penchant for shortbread.

SET YOUR TABLE

If you are going to superimpose a photo of yourself with the Queen, make it a good one.

Field of Screams

As I tried to resuscitate the fallen flamingo, I told myself perhaps I wasn't cut out for this assignment. Up until this unfortunate incident, I had successfully handled other complex situations—I taught college freshmen who were more interested in text messaging than American history. I re-wrote an entire magazine feature after my computer crashed. I even helped my children with their science fair projects, a feat that will test anyone's emotional mettle. Yet, nothing had prepared me for this. I was facing my ultimate challenge—chaperoning an elementary school field trip.

This experience entailed refereeing three precocious 7-year-old boys at a state park. After assigning them to me, the teacher quickly ran away, laughing and smiling like a person who suddenly feels free or something. I didn't see her the rest of the day, but I did witness dear William, one of my charges, bean a flamingo square in the middle of the eyes with a rock. I should've sworn off field trips right then as the poor pink creature went flat to the ground. And that was just the first five minutes of the day.

Ever the optimist, I volunteered to go on another adventure, this time to a local natural attraction theme park. Admittedly, while there were other things I'd rather do, I knew I would enjoy the time with my daughter and some of her 24 classmates who wanted to show me that their visible sinus infections were only viral, not bacterial. I never realized there are varying degrees of green on a Kleenex. This is just one of the jewels you discover on a field trip.

By the time we reached the boat cruise portion of the trip, the group was tired, grumpy, and hungry. And the children were getting restless, too.

Captain Jim, a robust fellow in his khaki captain's uniform, barked a few orders to his new crew about staying alert and looking out for danger. Little Timmy tried to show him how a Gummi Bear would stick to his front tooth, but the Captain was unwavering in his focus. He had a boat to guide.

Beside him lay a mysterious burlap bag that the Captain tightly held onto as he steadied the boat for departure. His second in command, Fred, pushed the boat away from the dock.

That's when it happened.

While pushing from the dock, Fred fell off the boat and into the gator-infested waters. Captain Jim leapt across the children and went into rescue mode. As he jumped into the water, an interesting choice of words poured out of the Captain's mouth.

"Oh, $#%*! We've got a man down! We've got a man down! Oh, $#%*!

I hadn't seen the kids so wide-eyed since the time their teacher forgot to wear a slip to school one day.

Then the burlap bag came to life and the children began to scream.

"Mrs. Mangan! There's a snake in the bag! Aaaaaaaaaah!"

And indeed there was. A very big snake. Sitting right beside me, slithering out of the burlap bag. The boat started rocking from all the commotion as the teachers tried to calm down the children and the parents. Fortunately, Captain Jim swam back to the boat with Fred, grabbed the snake, and restored order, although young Suzie asked the Captain what $#%* meant, so that was a little awkward.

At that moment, I decided maybe my volunteering skills are better used elsewhere—like in an office or a classroom or a closet. Anywhere that doesn't involve wounded flamingos or loose snakes.

SET YOUR TABLE

Field trips? Skip it if a boat, snake, and poor swimmer as your guide is involved.

A MOMENT WITH
Grace Hamlin

Lifestyle blogger and influencer Grace Hamlin follows her heart when shopping. Grace's home features layers of wicker and rattan, mixed with warm tones, right alongside bright white lacquer and maybe even some acrylic or Lucite. Throw in some needlepoint touches and sentimental tchotchkes and she's especially happy.

Q: Any guiding principles you follow in your work?
Grace: Trust your gut. Especially when we're talking about shopping at thrift stores, consignment stores, or flea markets, you can't really wait around and

@GraceHamlin

mull it over because otherwise it'll be gone! I've never regretted the times I followed my gut.

Q: Do you have a sentimental accent piece that's a favorite?
Grace: My grandmother's framed business card! Growing up she'd tell me all about her store that she had many years ago, Sir Drake's Gifts for Men. I loved that she saw a need—thoughtfully curated gift store for men—and went for it. I loved how she lit up when she talked about that time in her life. When she passed away, I knew instantly I wanted to frame one and hang it.

Q: What does home mean to you?
Grace: Home is synonymous with a sense of belonging. More than order and organization, what I hope is that in their own home my children feel that what is important to them is also important to me. At the end of the day, as hard as we work to create places and spaces that are beautiful and comfortable, what matters most is the people who fill them.

SET YOUR TABLE
Take a vintage shopping trip and trust your purchasing instincts. Choose items you'll use, but also feel special.

The Road of What Ifs: A Birthday Reflection

Not too long ago, I passed a car with a license plate that read "WHATIF." I've always been struck by those who have tags like "360 GUY" ("All Around Guy," get it?) or EDUGATR (not as clever, but more so than my tag's I.D. with random numbers I can't remember when asked to provide them on a registration form.) I really wondered: What was the WHATIF driver trying to convey?

Maybe he was part of a national introspective movement that sold bumper stickers and T-shirts with "What If?" stamped in bold letters. Perhaps a rock-the-universe pivotal moment in his life gave said driver enough pause to ponder the meaning of it all so he quit the 60-hours-a-week job, ditched the unhappy relationship and hopped on the interstate for a life-changing road trip.

Seems to me, requesting this turn of phrase at the tag office is a very intentional act.

Maybe he just wanted to prod other drivers to ask the same question. If so, permission requested.

Middle age introduced me to "What if."

I never thought much about the untraveled roads of life until I turned 40, because I was **a)** too caught up in life's whirlwind of high school, college, first job, marriage, first home, babies, seconds on college, job, home and babies; **b)** rich with self-projected certitude about my choices; **c)** immortal; and **d)** completely full of hooey about b and c.

Looking back on the choices of my youth, I realize how absolutely youthful I was.

What if I made a wrong career choice? Who cares? I have the rest of my life for a new start. What if I lost touch with a close friend? I'll reconnect when life is calmer. What if I never followed my passion to be a Big Band singer? I'll sing when I retire at my oceanfront home with the recording studio.

You know the rest of the story, the chapter with the real answers. You know because you've lived it, too. You've asked "What if?" You've lived with "What now?" I have as well, often finding the re-written chapters—the ones edited with unexpected narrative—to be more beautiful, more fulfilling, than the original (cue Garth Brooks' "Thank God for Unanswered Prayer").

But, we know too well the other part of the story. The chapter of unrealized dreams. Hopefully, we'll have time for a few "do overs."

Yet, it's the non-refundable part of "What if?" that gets to me lately. I know of families right now hurting with unexpected losses of loved ones. They thought they had more time. May they find comfort in knowing their "What if" checklist was full of memories of love and happiness and, most importantly, togetherness. No one ever regrets asking "What if I hadn't spent so much time with those I loved?"

The driver sped ahead of me. I couldn't see where he was heading. I drove slowly behind him humming Frank Sinatra until the car faded over the hill.

SET YOUR TABLE

Instead of what if, focus on what is.

Facebook's Four Stages of "This Can't Be"

I have mixed emotions about Facebook's memory reminders, the posts where the social network site shows photos and events from users' past. "On this day, nine years ago, here's where you were, Amy Yeary Mangan!" exclaims Facebook with attached photos of the referenced day. Inevitably, when this notice pops up on my feed, I get an overwhelming sense of nostalgia combined with a whopping heart pang. I think I'm suffering from the Four Stages of This Can't Be.

Stage One: Denial. Last week, Facebook's memory moment showed a post I made four years ago when I was leaving my oldest on the footsteps of the college dorm for the first time. What happened to the last four years? Poof.

Stage Two: Regret. I admit it. Some of these posts make me wonder "What if?" What if life could have been different for beloved friends and family members shown in my memory posts? Could life have been different for me?

Time waits for no one and neither does disappointment and heartache. Every single person in my posts has experienced both because this is the prickly/lovely dichotomy of being an earth dweller. We've all suffered devastating losses and painful lessons, a reminder how quickly life can go from blissful contentment to mind-numbing shock in a nanosecond, or, in this case, a Facebook feed.

It's the old "if I knew then what I know now" reflection. Would I have done anything differently if I could? Sometimes the answer is yes. Yes, I would've made time for coffee with my friend who is no longer here. Yes, I would've gone on that trip I begged off for some big ole' important reason I fail to remember.

Knowing what I now know, would I have slowed down and just enjoyed the here and now, which, in the post, was then and there? Oh yeah.

Funny, but there isn't a single post of me in front of my computer, an almost constant appendage.

Stage Three: Humbled. It's not all morose. If you just went on the number of photos I've posted of celebrations, you'd surmise I'm one big partier. And, in a way, I guess I am, but not the pub-crawling kind (thankfully, social media didn't exist when I was in college).

Most of my feeds are celebrating special moments—graduations, engagements, babies, birthdays, fundraisers and, of course, Betty Cakes. I really like Betty Cakes, the local café with deliciously addictive cakes. Lots of posts of my favorite Betty Cake. Judging by my frequent posts, I also like lemon drop martinis, especially with friends. And how great is that? The older I get, the more profoundly appreciative I am for these times, big, small and delicious.

Stage Four: Ready. Here's what I know: It does me no good to get hung up on what I didn't do or should have done, or wish would have never happened. I've come to accept these posts as emotional instructive. When a one appears—"On this day, two years ago, Amy Yeary Mangan, here's where you were!"—I lean back, soak in the photo and utter a quiet "Thank you" beneath my breath. Thank you for this memory. And for the reminder that it's time for me to take a computer break.

Because on this day, I've got a life inviting me to make some new memories.

SET YOUR TABLE

Thank you is always the right answer.

September

Centerpieces: Pace

To me, September is the ultimate pre-game before the rush of what comes next. Each year I vow to create holiday menus in advance so I'm not rushing to the grocery store the night before a big meal, scanning empty aisles for crushed pecans. I also like to draft a gift list with thoughtful presents. I've fallen into the gift card habit so, once again, committing to limit the plastic purchases.

Growing up, Mama had a gift closet where she stored collections of random items optimal for sharing when the need or party arose. I've continued this tradition in every home I've owned, even the tiny apartment rental where my gift closet was a drawer. The gift inventory process is more intentional now. I have dedicated shelves in my home office closet where I store presents with sticky notes attached with the recipient's name, lest I forget. If, and this is a *big* if, I do it right this year, I will have completed shopping before the Macy's Day Thanksgiving Parade. A girl has gotta dream!

SET YOUR TABLE

Dedicate space and intention to your gift giving approach and don't forget the sticky notes

Looking at the Bright Side

Some disturbing news recently made headlines. Lightning bugs are on the decline. Several reasons were provided. Experts cited pollution, chemical pesticides and a change of natural habitat as to why we aren't seeing the luminescent insects as often. Scientists chimed in on what this means to our environment.

What this means to me is far more personal.

I'm losing a valuable parenting tool.

Last summer, my family and I were on vacation in Atlanta. My husband, Mike, and I took our children to dinner in the heart of the city, excited to snag a booth next to the window for optimal viewing of neighboring skyscrapers. Next comes the part of the story that is the honest truth (forgive the emphatic redundancy; it's a family trait that appears in moments of excitement).

Earlier that day in Atlanta, I lamented the fact I hadn't seen a lightning bug in a long time. My pre-teen kids asked, "What's a lightning bug?"

Dumbfounded, I told them about my childhood in the country, today's backside of our local mall. Just after dusk on most nights, my next-door friend and I rushed outside with empty mayonnaise jars to entice a few fireflies into our canisters. We'd quickly screw on the lids punctured with holes for adequate bug oxygen-intake levels. By supper time we parted company, glowing glasses in hand, giddy with our prizes.

When I headed to bed, I propped the jar on my windowsill.

Instant homemade LED camping light.

I drifted to sleep watching my glow-in-the-dark, darting polka dots.

The next day, the bugs were still buzzing around inside the jar but with a more frenetic, well, buzz. Dad walked into my room and asked me of my longterm intentions with my fluorescent friends. He asked how I'd like to be stuck in a jar on a shelf just within reach of outdoor freedom.

"But I like them," I told him.

More the reason, he said, to let them do what they do best outside the confines of a greasy container.

My oldest said that brought back memories of trying to keep some crickets inside a box, an action modestly depleting Central Florida's cricket population. Grif said we should let all living things live freely and in peace.

It was a teachable moment, an illumination of another kind.

Back at the Atlanta restaurant we were nibbling on bread rolls when my daughter let out a yelp. Outside our window, smack-dab in the middle of the Southern concrete jungle, was one very bright lightning bug twirling and leaping like a Cirque du Soleil acrobat.

My oldest said maybe this was the bug I released as a child.

Um, Maybe?

This very bright lightning bug, after all, proceeded to entertain us for the next few minutes with a dazzling aerobatic dance as if to say, "Hey, I'm just happy to be here no matter what the experts say!"

And we were happy to be there, too.

SET YOUR TABLE

If you find a firefly, enjoy the dance.

Faux Real

No shocker I like to decorate. I'm not an interior designer, but I know what I like and try not to impose my design preferences on others. Except for my friend Dave's recliner that he refuses to relocate. When I'm lucky, a friend will ask me for some home décor recommendations. This is my Christmas. I take pics of the focus area and cull ideas from stores, books, and magazines. If I'm in a creative spirit, I'll assemble this in a customized three-ring binder. Not that anyone asked for me to go to such lengths and, again, I bear no credentials besides being a certified home and garden freak.

My most recent decorating faux client was my friend Mary who had moved into an adorable cottage-styled home. We went to work, moving furniture, hanging pictures, adding accessories, and toasting our work with a glass of champagne. We first set up the dining room using her gorgeous cherry dining table and hutch. Mary loves all things blue and white, so, we accented the room with blue and white toile plates and vases. We added some family heirlooms and one standout capiz shell chandelier. The other night Mary texted me a pic of a blue and white rug she bought. Perfect! My work was done. She's on her way to make her home exactly what she wants it to be.

I'm currently accepting new faux clients to help them with free faux design services. Champagne optional. Who am I kidding? You may pay me in Chandon.

SET YOUR TABLE

Got a décor challenge? Start with one space a time and build your own notebook with rooms that you love. Go shopping in your own home.

Living Your Personal Yes

So I was e-mailing a few friends about getting together when a revelation occurred.

It was one of those "ah-ha" moments you hear about on Oprah but wonder if something like this ever happens to mere cash-strapped mortals who don't spend much time thinking about "living their best lives" by ascribing to self-help philosophy because they are too busy, well, living their lives, best or not.

The more I think about it, the more I see how flawed the situation was.

How it was so perfectly set up for failure.

Yes, failure.

Indeed, it's so clear now, looking back.

The picture is coming into focus.

I'm beginning to see the light (cue the orchestra or, for that matter, any Joni Mitchell song).

I'll cut to the end first. My friend's e-mailed reply was "No." She diplomatically declined getting together, saying she just couldn't take on one more thing.

Whoa. One more thing? Since when is having fun with friends considered one more thing?

I'll tell you when.

It's when your overscheduled exhausted Blackberry is overloaded to the point you can't add alarms for more meetings so you won't forget them or else your whole day will be ringing.

It's when you've maxed out your emotional Palm Pilot so much you can't stop sobbing over an "Extreme Makeover" that aired three days ago. And everyone on the show was still living. It was one of those bonus episodes.

It's when, between being wife/husband, mom/dad, daughter/son, friend/acquaintance, co-worker/boss, volunteer/leader, you crawl into bed, bone tired, can't even read one page in your book without nodding off. You simply collapse. With the lights left on. In your work clothes.

It's when you call the vet to make an appointment for your dog and the receptionist reminds you, ever so gently, that you just brought Fido in two weeks ago, don't you remember? Then, she asks sweetly in a lyrical and youthful voice because she is young and probably sleeps eight hours a night,

"Do you have another Fido who needs his shots?"

No, honey. Just a worn-out middle-aged mama who needs somethin' stronger than a shot, thank you.

Oh, were we talking about my friend?

What's wrong with this picture? One more thing?

I so get that.

Why was I e-mailing instead of picking up the phone to call my friends? Here's what's more shameful: It wasn't even a personal invitation. I was asking my friends to attend an event for my job.

Revelation time.

When my friend sent her reply, I got it. Truly. Good for her. Because her "no" was really a "yes" to self-preservation.

Yes to minimizing the overload. Yes to fewer obligations.

We should each try to live more of our "personal yes" this year. Wouldn't that be nice? Hey, I like that. Living our yes is living our best.

Oprah, are you listening?

Nahhh. She's probably too busy.

SET YOUR TABLE
Sometimes yes is better than no.

Meaning of Correspondence

It's that time of year when I begin thinking about holiday cards. These past few years, I've skipped sending them. This is kind of a big deal because, if you know me, you know that this seasonal tradition is right up there with my fondness for HGTV, LhasaPoos, and Hungry Bear's corn nuggets. I also adore receiving cards—so much, in fact, that I've kept decades of them in a basket that I pull out every December and place on the coffee table.

This year, I decided to dust off my old mailing list and send a card. Scrolling through my contacts, I was quickly reminded not only of the joy-affirming presence of loved ones in my life, but also of those who are no longer here.

My children's pediatrician.

My friend's sweet husband.

The former neighbor who carpooled the kids to school.

My nephew.

My father.

My beloved aunt, the one who had already bought my birthday gift—an angel ornament—a month ahead of time before she unexpectedly passed.

My sister-in-law who loved scented candles almost as much as her King Charles Spaniel, husband and daughters.

The co-worker whose life was cut short.

My mother-in-law who shared my affinity for Red Lobster's cheesy biscuits.

It was such a somber punch in the gut that I took a break to recollect myself. Yes, life is fleeting. We know this right? Yet, it's a truth that's easy to forget or intentionally ignore. Add all the Christmas good cheer, holiday commercials with too-perfect families and Michael Bublé and it's almost too much.

Returning to my desk, I did a perspective check. My goodness, I've lost more friends and family than I thought would occur at this juncture in my life. Then again, I'm not as young as I think or feel. How'd that happen? Well, life happened. And if you're lucky enough to escape pain and loss then you're... um, not human.

I find myself thinking how I wished I'd spent more time with those whose names on my list have an ominous delete checkmark next to them. Of course, they're never really gone. They are present everywhere I turn with emotional triggers that elicit memories:

When I hear Dave Matthews on the radio, I think of Josh, my nephew.

When I put the angel ornament on my Christmas tree, I think of Aunt Clovis.

When I celebrate my friend's birthday, I think of her husband, a kind soul and skilled building contractor, who hung pictures in my home.

Each time I hear a really good jazz ensemble, Dr. John Brinsko is right next to me in spirit.

Every single day when I see my father's red toolbox and published books beside my desk, I think of the one and only Sherman Yeary, author/contractor/ father extraordinaire.

Through the years, I've made plenty of excuses as to why I don't have time to send a holiday card. Then I remember how good it feels to be on the receiving end. After a busy day, it's a peaceful ritual to collect the unopened cards from the mail sitting on my table, find a comfy spot on the couch and read each card ever so deliberately.

I find these tidings truly comforting. For the love. For the experiences. For showing up. For hanging pictures plumb and centered.

So, I will send a card this year as a small way to return the favor, eagerly awaiting for the mail to arrive.

SET YOUR TABLE

Pour some wine when reading through the holiday cards. Reflect on the sender and what they mean to you.

Flannel Fashionista

Sleepwear has emerged as a major fashion trend. This is good news for me since I live in my favorite jammies until mid-afternoon most weekends. Yet, stylists are pushing the pajama boundaries, dressing their favorite model—aka one of Taylor Swift's best friends—in slinky negligees or robes and sending them out in public, as in out to dinner, out to a movie and out to the Met Gala. The latter to which, once again, I was not invited. Shocker.

This is bad news for me unless a sweatshirt and pants count for haute couture. I've never been a fashion goddess, but this latest fad seems to be a stretch.

Admittedly, this is coming from the woman who wears a cotton night shirt purchased during the Reagan years. Floral nightgowns with smocking will make a comeback, just you wait.

So, I'm a little sleepwear challenged. All this pajama fuss stirs up a painful memory.

When pregnant with my daughter, I was on medical bed rest for 12 weeks.

My doctor mandated restricted activity, limiting my productivity. I knew the key to my emotional sanity was to somehow stay busy. So, I rented a hospital over-bed table, churned out work and essays on my laptop and caught up on reading. I even re-arranged my bedroom thanks to patient family and friends who moved the dresser and TV stand at the direction of the pregnant woman barking orders from the comfort of her mattress.

Soon after I was put on bed rest, I found out my daughter was breech and would require a Caesarean birth, not my preference, but the best and safest choice. Preparing for surgery once I made it to 36 weeks pregnant, I used my bed-turned-command-center to study up on C-sections and post-surgery healing. I called other moms to set up my 2-year-old child with play dates after mama and newborn little sister came home from the hospital. I made a meal schedule for my husband and hired a painter to finish my oldest's new room since baby girl was getting the nursery. I even finished a couple of long-term work projects in advance.

However, what I failed to do was pack a decent-looking pair of pajamas for my hospital stay. Not once did I think about what I'd wear in the hospital, which was a foregone conclusion where I would end up. Granted, in the grand scheme of things, this wasn't a priority, but, I kind of had a heck of a lot of time on my hands in my bedroom boardroom.

Which is why the first photo of me holding my newborn daughter in my hospital bed has me attired in what can only be best described as nightwear for a lumberjack. The woven wool nightgown looked like the worst version of a tartan with red, green and blue criss-crossed lines, like Clan of the Can't-You-Do-Better?

No lovely pale-pink Grace Kelly-esque two-piece with matching furry slip-on slippers for me. Nuh-huh, honey, give me flannel and lots of it. I don't recall owning that gown. Maybe I bought it online when the only online options were poorly designed pajamas? www.plaidpjs.com?

So, it's safe to say you won't see me out and about in a silk slip dress, nor flannel nightgown. I'd like to think this is my gift to humanity, sparing shame and wool fabric for none to see.

SET YOUR TABLE
Ditch the flannel. 'Nuff said.

Slow Going Toward the Glass Menagerie

A chance encounter with a glass sliding door gave me a wake-up call. Story set-up: I live in a house that has interior sliding glass doors—lots of them. Doors to the dining room. To the family room. To the kitchen. So, it would be easy to, say, bump into one. Trouble is, I didn't just bump, I crashed head-first into the glass. The impact was so strong and loud I was certain I had shattered the door. Or my head.

Thankfully, both remained intact though I had a heck of a bruised forehead.

When I was finally able to stand up without seeing little white lights (this really does happen after full impact. Who knew?), my husband put his hands on my shoulders, looked me square in the eyes and said firmly, "Slow down."

Sage advice. It wasn't like I was rushing to put out a kitchen fire. Where was I going with such a robust sense of urgency? To the family room. To sit. On the couch.

Slowing down doesn't come easy; not only for me, but also for many other distracted rushers.

A whole "slow movement" is gaining attention, encouraging us to change our fast-paced lives and connect to something real—like family, friends and the good earth. Though we already may make these kinds of connections, the slow-goers contend we often do so while preoccupied with items that are less real.

Technology is a big culprit. How often have you asked someone to put down the cell phone, laptop or iPad while eating a meal together or having a conversation? Or someone has asked you to do the same?

I witnessed a scene with a young family at the beach. The children were doing handstands in the shallow part of the ocean, laughing as the crashing waves interrupted their acrobatics. This went on for some time. They'd turn back to the shore yelling for their parents to watch. Mom and Dad missed it all, nose deep into their tablets and cell phones.

Here's the thing: I don't want to rush through life. Contrary to the bruised bump on my head, I prefer living in the slow lane.

Technology is seldom my Achilles heel. It's my brain that I have a hard time turning off.

My accident was more a result of being mentally distracted than sprinting to claim the soft spot on the couch. I was deep in thought about who-knows-what when I became one with the door.

Aside from the honorable intentions of the slow movement, our culture encourages us to perform at full-speed. Take on another assignment. Volunteer for an additional committee. Respond to an untenable number of emails.

A multi-million dollar industry of planners and online organizers exist solely because we believe we need a system to stay ahead of ourselves. This seeps deep into our mental state, rendering it difficult to stop thinking about all the things we have to do. Next thing you know, your brain is on overload. Sometimes you run into doors. Or, worse: you're stopped cold from emotional and physical exhaustion.

Wouldn't it be great to change the more-is-better mentality on our life's resume to doing just a few things really well? Wonder how that would go in an interview?

"I do one thing brilliantly. And I pay attention to what and who really matters."

Our slow-moving friends believe this is possible. Baby steps. I'm trying to minimize my mental clutter and slow down and soak in what's around me. I don't want to crash into glass again anytime soon.

And I sure don't want to miss handstands in the ocean.

SET YOUR TABLE

Slow down. Repeat. Slow down. Rushing can hurt.

October

Centerpieces: Indulge

Not a Halloween goes by that I don't think of the mayor. Like most people of authority, he commanded any room he entered. One distinction: He wasn't the mayor. This was an honorary title bequeathed by my fellow neighbors and me.

Buzz was my neighbor three houses down and step-dad to a boy close to my oldest child's age. He welcomed us to the neighborhood with a bottle of wine, an offer to carpool the kids to their elementary school and a home renovation tip for my kitchen. I liked him from the start.

If you're lucky, you live in a place where someone serves as the communal glue. If there was a storm, Buzz alerted us to an emergency mustering plan should one of our houses be impacted. Early release day from school? Buzz covered it by picking up the neighborhood kids in his SUV and hosting an afternoon pizza and swimming party at his house. Monthly potluck neighborhood dinners? Bring yourself and a pot of good eats, Buzz would say.

A veteran, Buzz retired early and dove into other passions like renovating his home top to bottom and helping others any way he could. He lent a skilled hand on the kitchen remodel he convinced me to do.

Halloween was Buzz's sweet spot. You could count on him to rally the neighborhood troops for a fun night. We'd find a central location—someone's front yard—put up a tent, add a card table or two topped with a candy, fried chicken and beverages for adults and children alike. Then we let the not-so-spooky festivities begin.

We'd trick-or-treat and stop by the home of the actual Ocala mayor, E.L. Foster, who had a basket of Snickers waiting for the little ones and mini-wine bottles for the big ones. Each year, I arrived to sniff out the vino, itching to pull it out by the time I turned the corner toward the Fosters' house.

This got me thinking about a book I read a while ago—Robert Putnam's "Bowling Alone: The Collapse and Revival of American Community." Its premise is simple and relevant decades later: We are more disconnected than ever before. We bowl alone. We disengage from community organizations. Just look at Rotary National's membership numbers. Cultural changes in our lives contribute to this decline. Keep in mind Putnam wrote his societal analysis

18 years ago, long before social media rocked our world. He wrote that we, as a nation, are lacking in social capital, which leads to communal disconnect.

Lately, I've thought a lot about Buzz.

Tragically, he passed a few years ago. We had longed moved out of the neighborhood, but haven't replicated such an extraordinary sense of place. This week is a sobering reminder of all we have lost. I think of Mayor Buzz. In all the times we lived close by, we never spoke of politics, an oddity in this hyper-fueled political climate today. There were hints we may have sat on different political sides of the fence, but we were connected more by what bonded us than separated—love of family, community, each other.

The last Halloween we lived in the Mayor of 13th Street's district, I remember walking down the street to set up for the night. I brought cupcakes but forgot the paper plates at my house. When I turned to walk back to my house, Buzz stopped me to show he had an extra stash of plates beneath the table.

He looked out for me. For us. Like always.

SET YOUR TABLE

Who is the mayor of your neighborhood? Celebrate him or her for the sense of community created.

Hay Bales of Gratitude

A few years ago in early November, a gift was left on my doorstep. It was a bale of hay, tightly bound with string.

Some women get flowers, I get straw. Even though a note wasn't attached, I knew who was responsible. I had recently visited a friend's house and was bowled over by her harvest entrance that would make Martha Stewart swoon.

Her front door was surrounded by pumpkins and glorious sunflowers placed on top of a hay bale. She credited her husband, Karl, for the hay bale element. Well done, Karl. Well done. I complimented his hay selection, which was perfect, not over-the-top, but impactful. Like Macy's in New York City window-display impactful.

I love fall. It's my favorite season. And for many years, I tried to decorate my home accordingly. On the side table in my foyer, I'd bring out the miniature wooden pumpkins with pumpkin-shaped candies in the pumpkin-shaped candy dish next to the pumpkin-scented candle because I ascribed to the Pier One belief that you really can't have too much pumpkin. Yet my front door exterior just had a harvest wreath—with hot-glued mini pumpkins, naturally.

I felt something was missing, but what? Then I visited my friend.

It was the hay.

As I drove around town the next few days, suddenly all I could see were finely decorated front entries with hay bales. Where had hay been all my life? And where exactly does one go to secure a bale for non-agrarian purposes? I'm a city girl who lacked hay-purchasing prowess.

A week later I pulled into my driveway and there it was. My very own bale of hay. It was almost better than Christmas. Karl was my Hay Bale Santa.

I immediately went to work. Using the hay as my central focal piece, I added all the faux fall vegetables I could find at the craft store. My front entryway was enveloped in mustard yellow, burnt orange and burgundy squash, gourds and other undefinable produce (in the craft universe there oft exists a maroon vegetable).

Life forced us to downsize that spring, but the following fall another bale of hay arrived at my rental door. Then we had to move again. More straw followed. My Hay Bale Santa was persistent, following us from one rental to the next.

One move was particularly hard. In the aftermath of leaving our home where I received my first hay bale, my family was catapulted into the universe of the unknown. We had moved into a small apartment complex. Most of our remaining possessions were in boxes in the cramped laundry closet. Driving home from an out-of-town work meeting, I pulled into the city limits.

Neighborhoods were adorned with pumpkins and hay. That's when I remembered: It was fall. And I had forgotten. I'm sure those faux vegetables were somewhere in my boxes, but why bother? A bale of hay would look silly on my Lilliputian apartment doorstep.

Then I pulled into the complex parking lot. And there it was—a bale of hay, but not just any bale of hay—a miniature hay bale perfect for a tiny doorstep. Running through the door, I yelled for the kids to grab the maroon vegetables. Hay Bale Santa had struck again! It was time to decorate.

This week is our season of gratitude. I don't know if Santa Karl knew of my personal challenges through the years, but I suspect he did. And each time I see a bale of hay, I think of how a simple gift of straw made my load a little lighter.

Well done, Karl. Well done.

SET YOUR TABLE

A hay bale just may be the best Fall gift ever. Spread a little Fall love with a bale for a friend.

Sometimes the Biggest Thrill is Standing Tall

I spoke to a man who is planning to fall from the sky. He's taking his daughter with him. Her 18th birthday is coming up and she asked to go sky diving so, being the cool/insane dad this man appears to be, he's jumping, too. When I turned 18, I asked my parents for a fake opal ring from Service Merchandise and permission to go to a midnight movie. Yeah, I'm an adrenaline junkie from way back.

Thrill seeking is not in my DNA. I have no desire to dive from the clouds or climb a mountain that's too tall and dangerous for its own good. As a toddler, I remember taking swimming lessons with a visibly frustrated swim teacher trying to pry my chubby fingers away from the Styrofoam floating board. I wasn't letting go. I saw what happened to poor little Janice in the shallow end next to me. She let go of the board and sunk like a concrete block until her mom—fully clothed—jumped in as the teacher rolled her eyes.

Yet I admire those who take big chances in the air or on the ground. Such gumption! They move across the country or world for a new opportunity, redefine their identity, explore a new passion or try something new just because.

I have not strayed too far, still living in my hometown. I once rode a helicopter over the jagged cliffs of the Nā Pali coast and promptly kissed the Hawaiian terra firma when we landed.

A few years ago, I watched the chilling "Man on Wire" documentary about tightrope walker Philippe Petit's 1974 high wire routine performed between the World Trade Center's twin towers. Watching his first tentative step on the wire was as gut-wrenching as it was exhilarating. Petit did this illegally while NYPD hesitantly closed in on him since the police force was short on tightrope cops.

Everyone kept asking Petit why he did this daring act in New York City. "There is no why," he replied.

Now that I'm older, I realize I may have missed a few invitations to push myself, though I've been nudged and pushed in ways I never imagined.

There have been days when it felt like I was falling from the sky without a parachute. I've experienced adventures not of my asking, a common denominator for us all, really. Health scares, broken relationships, financial uncertainty, losing someone we love—it can be a scary freefall. This is when we have to let go of what we know and jump into what we must do. We find ourselves on the rope, gingerly assessing the next step while grasping for anything to hold onto for balance. I guess this requires a steely kind of gumption, too.

Sometimes we fly because we have to. Sometimes there is no "why."

I can beat myself up all day on adventures I did not take. But I try to look at the chances I took and the ones I had to take to survive or help someone I love make it through a frightening time in the inky dark clouds of the unknown. It's an emotional kind of sky diving.

For nearly an hour, Petit bounced and pivoted 110 stories above New York City. At one point, he leaned down and sat on the wire, saluting a stunned crowd below. He had this child-like grin, like "I did it!"

Adventures come in many forms, some of our choosing, some not. It's good to stop and salute the fact we're still standing and willing and, maybe, jumping.

SET YOUR TABLE

Yes, there can be reward with risk. What is yours?

Listless and Love it

After the hustle and bustle of the holidays, it's nice to enjoy a little less hustle. Actually, it's more than nice.

It's downright blissful.

Maybe this is middle age or the escalated carb intake talking, but, right now, nothing makes me happier than, well, nothing. More specifically, doing nothing.

And, judging from the results of a highly technical survey I recently conducted (i.e. friends, family and strangers at the grocery store), doing nothing these days is, quite possibly, the best gift of all.

I think of the cartoon that depicts a couple standing at the end of a rainbow next to a golden pot with the words "Baked Beans" painted on it.

"Quite frankly," says the man to the woman, "I'm a bit disappointed."

This year—2008—was a bit disappointing, wasn't it?

Sure, if you look closely, beyond our country's economic free fall, escalating national debt, ongoing global fill-in-the-blank war/warming/financial crisis, we can find pockets of hope.

Paris Hilton hasn't been in the news for the past 48 hours. And, joy of all joys, I finally figured out how to de-frag my computer. I feel so Bill Gate-ish.

Some happiness and progress took place this past year, but goodness gracious, it was hard earned.

A friend cautioned me not to wish a year away; however, I'm ready for something new.

So, I'm tweaking my expectations for my new year's resolutions.

I'm not making any. (See how fun doing nothing can be?)

This was a tough decision.

Those who know me know I am a list maker. I'm the one whose mantra is "Order breeds serenity." (Husband, quash thine urge to add "and insanity, too.")

Lists make me happy.

Some women read fashion magazines, I pour over the latest Franklin Covey catalog.

Jimmy Choos ain't got nothin' on the latest day planner.

Stillettos versus Palm Pilot? No brainer.

Still, a curious thing happened on the way to maximum efficiency: life.

While I can tick away a few cherished personal and professional accomplishments realized this past year—admittedly, due most likely to some degree of organized focus—I'd like to explore a different path.

Something more fluid, less structured.

I believe, and perhaps you, do, too, we have entered a time in which we may all be better served by welcoming a little more fluidity in our lives.

Resolutions infer expectations no matter what Oprah says. Once, after going on a self-help reading binge, I taped my resolutions to my bathroom mirror. Three months later after too much shower moisture, my list was droopy and withered, a metaphor if there ever was one.

This reminds me of the fortune teller who cautioned, "Don't get your hopes up. The future isn't what it used to be."

After collapsing on the couch the night of Christmas with no future agenda in sight, I asked my husband what was his favorite moment of the day.

He replied, "This."

I couldn't agree more.

SET YOUR TABLE

Go listless for a bit. You just might love it.

@mcleod_ashton

A MOMENT WITH
Ashton McLeod

"I love any space that is functional but also has an air of whimsy and pay particular attention to floral design, lighting and scents."

Doesn't that just sound lovely? I caught up with Ashton McLeod, an Ocala gal living in NYC, and asked her a few questions about what inspires her home!

Q: Do you have a current or sentimental accent piece that's a favorite?
Ashton: I have a painting that is the focal point of my living room, and I bought a white/reclaimed wooden desk to complement that painting by a dear friend

Isadora Capraro, an artist from Argentina. The painting is titled "Sailing Brings Me Peace" and is from her yoga series titled 'Asanas'.

Every morning, I write in my journal at the desk under the painting and also buy seasonal flowers each week that complement its vibrant colors.

Q: What does home mean to you?
Ashton: As someone who travels and is out at restaurants a lot for my career, I always look forward to going home. I refer to my home in Chelsea as my

'nest' where I replenish and nourish both my mind and body. My home is an extremely comfortable and warm space with accents of whimsy sprinkled in with book design, candles, delicate light fixtures and flowers/plants in every room. It's essential to me that I feel like I have a peaceful oasis that is my own amongst the busy city. It's also a space that I spend quality time cooking for my friends, so it's very grounding.

My mom's backyard is an absolute sanctuary of greenery and birds. With my apartment, I try to evoke a similar feeling and it reminds me of my family in Florida.

SET YOUR TABLE

Let art serve as your starting point for decorating a room.

Listening Party

Love music? Love friends? Host a Listening Party like Mike and I did complete with a turntable that I gave Mike as a gift. Invited guests brought their favorite album of all time, hidden in a paper bag until we guessed who brought what. We played, danced, indulged in a few music-themed "Let's Get Fizzical" cocktails and took a stroll down a musical memory lane.

SET YOUR TABLE

Host a listening party and the more music puns the better.

I AM THE HUMMUS

LET'S GET FIZZICAL

November

Centerpieces: Embrace

Jessie works at the St. Regis Bar after an 18-month pandemic break. She was as excited to be there as I was to be visiting my daughter and her boyfriend who live in the city.

"All of our staff is thrilled to be back," she said as she offered us the historic bar's iconic espresso martini. I asked her to take a snapshot to capture this moment. She agreed on one condition.

"Don't look at the camera," she said holding my phone.

Before we could respond, she quickly snapped a pic catching us mid-laugh thinking of the notion of us as social media influencers posing-not posing.

"That's the look I saw when I came up to your table for the first time," she said smiling, "And the look I try to remember of all my guests on our first weekend back."

SET YOUR TABLE

This season, snap some candids for life-affirming keepsakes.

Someone Left the Cake Out in the Rain

For the first time ever, I baked a cake. Not just any cake. I've baked that kind many times. This one was different. And it was an epic fail. I couldn't be prouder.

Backstory: My daughter is an epileptic, and she's been seizure-free for three years. While she has weaned down from five anti-seizure medicines to two, she would, ultimately, like to be med-free. The Ketogenic diet has proven successful for many who have her condition. So, Gilly—determined and doggedly optimistic—is trying the diet as a precursor to future medicinal reductions.

Being Keto means you follow a customized high-fat, adequate protein, low-carb diet. This is not an endorsed Keto commercial. I've now explained all that I know even after reading three books by doctors, nutritionists and Keto followers. By mid-point in my reading I think, "Man, I'd love some French Fries."

But it was Gilly's 22nd birthday. She was hosting a cook-out at her apartment with her friends. And she actually wanted her mom and dad to be there. She had the menu planned and said she was making a Keto cake.

Hold on! I'll make that cake, missy.

Like most things in life, that which is most rewarding is seldom simple. It didn't help that I was dealing with some stressors—a difficult work project, some personal matters and the election recount were mental disrupters to my baking soul. All factors led me to ignore the intricacies of making a cake that required ingredients I've never used before.

Still, I channeled Ina Garten, the queen of the baking universe, and thought, "What would Ina do?" Why, she would mix some stevia with almond flour into a "how easy is that?" baking pan and serve it to her husband, Jeffrey, and actress Jennifer Garner.

Yet, even this recipe would test Ina's baking chops. Turns out almond flour doesn't rise because, let's be honest here, it's not flour. And the buttercream icing was made of buckets of butter, which, butter being butter, melted in the sun. I threw some chocolate chips on the cake's top for aesthetic effect rendering a finished product that looked like a chocolate chip flat pancake swimming in yellow lava.

But, miracles happen when you are surrounded by grace.

Lucky for me, I was surrounded by cook-out guests with generous hearts and a birthday girl with the biggest heart of all. So, it didn't surprise me that Gilly loved the cake. So much, in fact, that she encouraged her friends to try a piece and graciously join in on the Great Keto Cake Tasting Test (Food Network, here's your new television program. You're welcome). The verdict? A greasy thumbs up with a recipe notation to serve with a spoon instead of a fork.

That day was never really about the cake. It was about celebrating my daughter. She has taught me so much about the value of being present. Of being mindful. Of not giving up. Of fighting through tough times while embracing the good.

Earlier that morning as I was making the cake, I caught myself paying attention to those stressors that were looping endlessly in my head. My heart began to pound with worry. Then I looked down at the bowl of eggs, almond "flour" and other ingredients that don't belong in a cake. Taking a deep breath, I said a prayer of gratitude that I was making something for someone so courageous, kind and open.

When I took the cake out of the oven, it looked nothing like the photo on the recipe, but it looked exactly like love.

SET YOUR TABLE

Just make a damn regular cake with regular flour.

Old but New

Speaking of pinching pennies, I snagged an epic find at my friend Susan's vintage store. The china hutch had seen a lot of living when I spotted the glass-paneled cherry cabinet at her warehouse. I needed somewhere to store my ever-expanding bar since Wedgwood takes second place to Tito's around here. Susan and her talented mom, Meta, refinished it with an onyx high gloss for the exterior and a light shade of robin's egg blue. I added a few brushed gold knobs and placed it in our kitchen, all for a fraction of what I'd pay retail. Even better is how much we love and use our converted hutch-turned-bar. To me, bringing new life to a worn object is more satisfying than buying new. Restoration is good for furniture and humans alike.

SET YOUR TABLE

Vintage pieces are (a) cheaper than online big box stores and (b) have more character just waiting for attention. Find one and show a little love.

@sage_house_farm

A MOMENT WITH
Crystal Flynn

Meet Crystal Flynn. Isn't her styling stunning? I love how she created a cozy, welcoming brunch tablescape using a mix of her vintage plates, her mother's silver, collected vintage linens plus a few of my personal favorite goodies. Her preferred aesthetic is blending the old and new… marrying primitive and classic.

"...your home should be a reflection of you."

Q: What is your favorite kind of space to design?
Crystal: Making gathering spaces in my home cozy is my favorite thing!

Q: Any guiding principle you try to follow in your design work?
Crystal: Be careful following trends—your home should be a reflection of you. Blending your tastes with seasonal trends is the best approach, in my opinion.

Q: What does home mean to you?
Crystal: My home is my refuge… where I reconnect with my family, recharge and create!

Q: Anything else you'd like to include about yourself?
Crystal: The only thing I love more than finishing and decorating this home we've built is cooking for my favorite people. There's just nothing better than gathering around a table and enjoying a meal together.

Why I Believe in Phone-Loving Millennials

For those who lament the seemingly self-absorbed behaviors of the American millennial, I offer a story of hope, one founded on the virtue of the cell phone, as paradoxical as that may seem.

Like most parents, I swallowed my heart when I dropped off my youngest to begin her freshmen year in college. This wasn't my first rodeo. My oldest was starting his junior year at another university, so, naturally, I thought I had this baby-bird departure thing figured out. Then I looked into my daughter's wide eyes as she stood in her dorm hallway. She looked so ready to fly.

"Don't worry, Mama," she said hugging me once more, her voice breaking ever so slightly. "I'll be OK. I'll be safe."

How young they all look, I thought, driving away from campus, gingerly navigating around baby birds on scooters and sidewalks as they talked on their cell phones.

"Pay attention!" I said aloud.

Gilly's first month went well. She made new friends, many whom I got to know via Facetime, a technological cell phone phenomenon I eventually learned to master.

Maddie, Kaley, Taylor, Bailey U., Gio, Hunter, Marshall, Ashley and a dozen others who graciously welcomed Gilly's mom into their bright and vibrant circle.

"Mama Mangz!" they'd shout as their fuzzy faces appeared on my phone's screen.

"Do you like my costume?"

Suddenly, I was a costume-design consultant. A toga? Thumbs down. Super Hero costume? Thumbs up. Then I became Dr. Laura.

"What? He won't pay for dinner?" I asked insistently on the phone. "Drop him!"

How lovely they'd include me, I'd often think—me, a middle-aged mama sitting on the couch wearing her Golden Girls sweatpants outfit, offering pithy advice.

Then, they helped me in ways I never imagined nor wanted.

One night just over a year ago, Mike and I had just sat down to enjoy our new empty nesters' dinner of Italian take-out. My cell phone buzzed as I was mid-bite into my lasagna. When I saw Gilly's name on the Caller ID, I answered and listened as she told me she'd had a good day. She raved about her cool poetry professor and how Taylor, her roommate, was so nice. Mike waited patiently for his turn to say hi. Gilly was telling me about her classes.

Then it happened.

Gilly let out a piercing moan, like a frightened, wounded animal trying to find shelter from the pain. The screeching howl was so profound, it stunned me for second.

The phone went silent.

I screamed into the phone.

I yelled her name again then handed the phone to Mike as if he could make her answer. Mike kept yelling her name into the phone, but I knew what had happened. The ugly beast of Gilly's epilepsy had resurfaced after a blissful quiet period of two years of being seizure free.

Somewhere in a city an hour away my daughter was having a grand mal seizure. I did not know where she was or who was with her, if anyone.

I tried not to imagine my sweet, daughter alone and unconscious, I called Taylor, Gilly's roommate. Taylor answered telling me she was at her sorority house and thought Gilly may still be in their dorm room.

"I'm running back right now!" Taylor said, already breathing into the phone in a fast sprint. "I'll find her."

And she did. And stayed by her as the EMTs lifted her into the ambulance.

So did several others of Gilly's friends during that time of darkness when Gilly had repeated seizures.

And you know what? That's not even half of it.

Gilly's friends became essential members of "Team Gilly." They took turns sleeping by her side. Driving her to dinner, the store, the library. Picking her up after her night classes to make sure she was never alone. They even celebrated her birthday with an innocent night of pizza and soda—no kegs for an epileptic—and stayed into the night to play one more round of cards.

It's been a journey since Taylor shattered Usain Bolt's record to rescue Gilly. She is better now. And yet, just a few weeks ago, she was boarding a bus to go to her first sorority dance.

That's when my cell phone began to buzz.

"Hey, Mama Mangz, we got Gilly covered," Kaley texted.

"Love you, Mama Mangz, checking in on behalf of Team Gilly," texted Emily with a photo of one gorgeous girl and her date.

"I'll make sure she takes her meds tonight," another chimed in.

The team has grown, too. Add Andrew and Bailey L. and Will and Caitlyn and Hailey and Emily and Louie to the list of "Really Cool Young Folk," as my mother would say.

It's not just how they care about my daughter, but how they care about the rest of the world. Ashley in Haiti. Bailey U. across the pond. Bailey L. helping those in need right here. Andrew G. in D.C. They volunteer. They work. Sometimes two jobs at once. They take damn hard classes. Spend college breaks in underprivileged countries.

They are remarkable. Compassionate. Engaged. Authentic. The realest of reals. If these millennials are any indication of our future, we're in good hands.

When they are ready to fly, it will be spectacular.

And we'll be OK.

SET YOUR TABLE

Hug the friends in your children's life. They may, literally, be lifesavers in unexpected ways.

Friendsgiving

I once had Eggs Benedict instead of turkey for Thanksgiving.

It was a Shoney's Restaurant special on the 10-dollars-and-under menu.

Lisa, who lived across the hallway from me in our dorm for graduate assistants, ordered the same thing. We split a large plate of greasy hash browns, our substitute for cornbread stuffing. An unorthodox holiday to be sure, but one I'll always remember.

With a major class assignment due the following week, I couldn't make it home for Thanksgiving. And, as a teaching assistant for the university's history courses, I had a pile of ungraded essays demanding to be read. Lisa was in the same boat. She was an English major, which meant she had twice as much writing and grading.

We made a promise to attack our class projects for the better part of Thanksgiving day. The payoff? A delicious turkey dinner at a restaurant of our choosing.

By 6 o'clock, Lisa tapped on my door.

"Let's eat turkey!" she exclaimed with the hunger of someone who had spent too much time parsing John Donne sonnets.

I grabbed my car keys and skipped down the stairs in anticipation of some major Tryptophan in my future. Lisa and I were giddy as we rattled off our favorite side dishes.

"Mac and cheese!"

"Corn pudding!"

"And bread!" I yelled with a little too much enthusiasm. "We must have bread!"

Ten minutes into our drive, it dawned on me I hadn't made reservations anywhere. Nor did I know what restaurants were open on Thanksgiving night.

Apparently, not too many.

This was, after all, nearly 30 years ago in a small city in the Florida panhandle. Even the Piggly Wiggly was closed that night. Forty-five minutes later, Lisa and I were still driving around like the couple of young, spontaneous students that we were. Who plans ahead? That's for old folks—you know, 30-year-olds!

An hour later and still no turkey. Lisa was biting her nails with the fervor of a grad student on the edge.

"I'm starving!" she yelled from her passenger seat. "Let's just go to a drive-thru."

"Absolutely not," I insisted with both hands gripped on the steering wheel like a madwoman on a mission. "We will not eat a hamburger tonight."

But, four miles later driving up and down a deserted highway, I was rethinking my position. So was Lisa. Turning to me, she gave me the look.

"You know what I'm thinking sounds good?"

Grinning, we nodded our heads.

"Eggs Benedict!" we declared.

Every Saturday morning, Lisa and I would make our weekly pilgrimage to Shoney's for their Big Breakfast All Day! special. Lisa was a Shoney's connoisseur. She knew every item on the menu and insisted their Eggs Benedict was the best around. She was right.

I came to love my Saturday breakfast with Lisa.

She and I were strangers when we arrived on campus a few months prior, both not knowing another person in the city where we had just moved. It was weird returning to college as a grad student. I suddenly felt old among the freshman running across the lawn for Greek Week. Then I met a 24-year-old English major living across the hall from me who loved Shakespeare and poached eggs drizzled in hollandaise sauce in equal measure.

I lost touch with Lisa a few years after we graduated. I've tried to find her on social media with no luck. She had dreams of being a college English professor out west. I only hope there's a Shoney's nearby.

Friendsgiving is trendy right now. Usually held before or after Thanksgiving, it is a celebration with friends in partial homage to the notion that friends are your family by choice. It is labeled as a new tradition, but I'd like to think I was partaking in friendsgiving a long time ago.

"To the best unplanned Thanksgiving ever!" I said as I tipped my sweet tea glass to Lisa's, grateful for a season in our lives that gave us each other and a meal worth savoring.

SET YOUR TABLE

Cast aside self-imposed ideas of what holidays are supposed to be and embrace the deliciousness of the atypical.

Thankful

Since this is a season of Thanksgiving and all things pumpkins, I decided to combine the two. On my kitchen counter sits my "thankful" pumpkin where family and friends pen in bold black Sharpie what they are thankful for. Good thing the pumpkin isn't real, thank you, craft store.

Each day I'm reminded how lucky I am to be among such thoughtful souls who share gratitude on a faux vegetable.

SET YOUR TABLE
Grab a fake pumpkin, a Sharpie and pen a few gratitudes.

December

Centerpieces: Celebrate

Thank goodness my sister Cindy keeps everything. Over the years, she drops off totes of my parents' belongings at just the right time. She's my own Google clairvoyant. A few holiday seasons ago, these exquisite coupe glasses found their way to me. Since my parents were Baptist teetotalers, the glasses were used for Mama's famous chocolate and pecan parfaits. Ready to restore them to their rightful purpose, Mike and I inaugurated the glasses with a bottle of Dom.

I rarely indulge in champagne except during the month of December, then, Santa better watch out! Most nights I play some holiday tunes, pour a glass of bubbly, light a few candles, and admire our Christmas tree from the comforts of the couch. I do believe this has come to be one of my favorite traditions of the season.

I also use this time to scan the daily entries in my journal, purveying a year of thoughts and emotions as I seek clues for modest epiphanies. Here's one: my daily gratitude list often includes the same events and people. Pups, too, of course! For years, this has been the pattern. What is interesting is what is not on the list—accomplishments or experiences I know took place, yet, failed to make the appreciation cut. Those that did are generally the quiet day-to-day activities that make up a life—long walks with Mike, Facetiming the children, a delicious dinner, catching up with friends, virtual movie nights, reading a good book, attending a concert, heck, even a cup of Earl Grey with honey was a repeater. And, yes, furniture made a regular shout out including my beloved abundance of tables.

It is a thankfulness for what brings me comfort and centers my soul and who ground me in love and wholeness. So the table series make complete sense because so much of this occurred around one of them, elbows on table, wine in hand, heart to heart. And that is why I celebrate the little moments that weave into the fabric of a life and time worth celebrating.

SET YOUR TABLE

Zoom in on your past year. Celebrate and savor who and what makes you grateful.

Mama's Pistachio Cake

Mama was known for her delicious pistachio cake and the icing is the perfect holiday color! Use a bundt pan for a Christmas wreath look if you like!

```
PISTACHIO CAKE              NELWYN YEARY

1 Box Duncan Hines White Cake mix
1 Box Pistachio INSTANT Pudding Mix
4 eggs
3/4 cup Crisco Oil
3/4 cup cold water
1 Teaspoon almond flavoring
Slight green food coloring if desired

Spray tube pan (or layers if desired) with Pam
Pre-heat oven 350 degrees

Beat with electric mixer eggs, oil, water flavoring, then add
cake mix and pudding mix.  Just a drop or two of green coloring
will do.  Beat until well blended, then beat well for 5 minutes.

Pour in pan, cook about 40 minutes or until it springs back when
touched.  Cool on wire rack.

Frost when cool with the following;

1 Box XXXX powered sugar
1 8 oz. cream cheese
1 stick oleo
1 cup cut up pecans

Blend oleo and cream cheese in electric mixer.  Add sugar,
flavoring and a drop or two of green food coloring until
well blended.
Fold in pecans.
Spread on cool cake.
```

Sticks of Love

One of the best presents I've received I gave to myself one week before Christmas. Then I gave it as a gift to someone else.

It was a bundle of branches; pussy willow stalks, actually. Not the real kind, the fake ones. They were 50 percent off at the local home décor store—an odd present at any time, let alone during a season of white lights and holiday cheer. Maybe that's why they were on sale.

I placed the branches into tall matching ceramic vases on either side of the fireplace in our living room. Since it was December, I added some faux holly berry ferns for a festive look, a clear affront to nature, but I loved it.

So did my nephew Josh. He was visiting from Jacksonville.

"I love your sticks, Aunt Amy," he said.

I wasn't going to parse the difference between sticks and stalks of beauty. I was thrilled someone noticed them, especially my 29-year-old nephew. Josh had recently purchased his first home a few blocks from the Atlantic Ocean.

Sitting on the brick lip of the fireplace in between my jolly holly-willow vases, Josh invited me to visit his new place. But, he laughed, I had to bring him some sticks.

Three months later, I visited Josh. I knew what was expected of me: fine looking sticks.

I searched local stores to find more, but they were gone. So I returned home, grabbed the stalks from my vases and headed to Jacksonville.

Josh gave me a tour of his home. He was so proud. I was, too. My nephew had blossomed into a successful young man running his own company while making a place for good friends and good times alongside the white-capped sea that fed his soul for surfing. He was charismatic and whip-smart funny, always making me laugh. Our tour ended in his family room where Josh declared the sticks would be prominently placed.

The story goes that pussy willows have legendary significance. They are viewed as harbingers of hope and prosperity. In early spring, the dry barren twigs bloom fuzzy white buds called catkins that look like tiny pieces of cone-shaped cotton. The Chinese believe the fuzzy buds signify wealth and abundance.

We hear a lot about prosperity these days. Headlines tell us the economic fog is lifting. Consumers are spending again. Retailers are optimistic about this holiday season, predicting what buyers want with such statistical accuracy they can identify how much each consumer will spend and what they will buy. There's something unnerving about a formulaic equation can predict what I will buy.

Trends, however, are made to be broken. My spending choices have changed significantly in the past few years. I shop less, and I've learned what to keep and what to give away. Like the pussy willows.

Josh died from an undetected heart condition two months after my Jacksonville visit. Eight years later, it's still hard to believe.

Life sometimes can be brutally barren with loss and grief. I now try to find harbingers of hope in the small things. Today, on this second day of December, Josh would have turned 38. And while his time in this world was abbreviated, Josh had an abundance of so much else: friends and family who adored him, a fulfilling job, and a welcoming home exactly where he wanted it to be.

I have curtailed my holiday shopping, instead focusing on spending time, not money, on what matters most to me. But I will never regret buying those sticks of love.

SET YOUR TABLE

Cherish loved ones. Make the effort. That is all there is, really.

Nancy With the Smiling Place

My introduction to film director Nancy Meyers came courtesy of a movie she directed about twin sisters separated at birth by their divorced parents. Just your typical love story.

She followed up with a film full of elegance, romance, and killer ocean views as in the Hamptons-inspired house that turned home design on its slipcovered head. Don't even get me started about her next film with Meryl Streep, Alec Baldwin and Steve Martin, another favorite that is on stand-by to play when I'm cooking.

While her plot narratives are compelling, I must confess it's everything else that has me hooked. Meyers' films drip with lifestyle ennui. The décor, the food, those muted ivory and khaki outfits accented with minimal, yet tasteful, jewelry. Meyers inspired middle-aged women across the land that our dreams were just within reach of a Williams & Sonoma. I even created a Spotify playlist of her soundtracks that I call "Nancy Meyers' Fangirl." Goes great with a crisp glass of Sauvignon Blanc and *Something's Gotta Give*.

These things I know for certain: I'll never have a terra cotta tiled residence on a sprawling Santa Barbara estate. Owning a French bakery is not in my future, nor is writing a Broadway play while sitting in my Hamptons home. I'd like to think this wasn't what Nancy was after. Rather, she created a space for grateful viewers to take a break from the madness of the day and escape. Which is exactly what I do.

SET YOUR TABLE

Promise to indulge in a Meyer's film and enjoy my "Nancy Meyers Fangirl" playlist.

Best Wedding Christmas Tree Ever

One of the greatest gifts I've received came in the form of a Christmas ornament; actually, about 50 of them. When Mike and I got engaged, the College of Central Florida (then known as CFCC), held a "Decorate Mike and Amy's Christmas Tree" party, a unique wedding shower to be sure.

We had several connections to the college. Mike was a CFCC Foundation board member and we were proud graduates of the college which, eventually, became my employer after graduate school. We were also an "older" betrothed couple; well, Mike more than I, of course. My fellow college employees wanted to ensure the imminent matrimony was adequately celebrated by throwing us a fabulous and festive shower.

Did they ever.

A month before our December wedding, the college cafeteria's conference room became Santa's Winter Wonderland. Bing Crosby crooned holiday tunes on the stereo while my colleagues busily channeled their inner elves serving punch and gingerbread cookies. There was just one request of guests—bring an ornament as a wedding gift.

Every ornament was beautiful and sentimental. Bunnies snuggling on a ceramic poinsettia from my friend Sandy, the animal lover. A gorgeous crystal obelisk from our stylish human resource director, Jan. A Santa Claus from our public relations specialist, Lisa, decked out in a sweater complete with jingle bells, who loved Christmas like an athlete. If holiday decorating were a sport, she'd would have won a gold medal.

Mike and I knew how lucky we were to be surrounded by friends who created such an incredible celebration of a special moment in time for us. This wasn't a new revelation, however. We knew this before the party. In work and life, we hit the trifecta in friendships. The pine-scented candles on the cafeteria tables was just icing on the cake, or snow on the tree, if you will.

I made so many declarations in my youth—full of what I would never do. Like never return to Ocala or marry anyone from Ocala. Or drive a mini-van. Or work at the same college from which I graduated.

Yeah, about that.

Somewhere along the way, I realized the beauty of what and who was around me. Thank goodness, Instagram wasn't around. That would've totally messed up a young and impressionable me thinking the great beyond was all that, well, great. Instead, all I needed to do was look around at who was right in front of me. Sane, talented humans who worked at a higher educational institution donning red reindeer noses that lit up as they greeted guests shouting, "Ho, Ho, Ho!"

Those, dear readers, were my people.

Luckily, I've stayed connected to many of them through the years. And every single Christmas, I am reminded of the kindred spirit of love when I pull out my holiday totes from the storage closet. One by one, I pull out an ornament and whisper a gratitude of thanks for the person who gave me this gesture of love.

There is one ornament that tugs at my heart—a wooden carving of two doves nestled with a dangling red heart beneath. This was from my friend Deb who bravely fought cancer more times than thought possible until she couldn't. She worked as an administrative assistant, more commonly known as the one who gets things done.

Gently, I place her ornament on my tree, remembering what she meant to me as well as my friends who cared enough to wear Santa Claus hats and red noses to commemorate an act of love which, by the way, they claim full responsibility for. Yes, the first time I met my husband was at a college meeting.

I guess you could say it was Kismet. Or, in our case, Christmas at a very special college.

SET YOUR TABLE

A holiday wedding shower is the best. Ever. Host one!

Good Lasso Tidings to You

'Tis the season for our annual neighborhood progressive cocktail party, and our dear friends Julee and Mike did not disappoint with their Ted Lasso-themed décor, meal and drinks. It was the perfect homage to the popular television show set in England —right down to the delicious shortbread biscuit and tea cocktail. However, the biggest win of the night went to Ted Lasso's iconic mustache. As guests arrived, Julee and Mike, decked out in soccer coach attire, instructed us to grab a 'stache and have some fun. What I believe they underestimated was just how much fun a stick-on mustache would bring to the six families who giggled and snapped selfies in the hallway until our hosts gently ushered us into dining room.

A perfect night with friends, family and a rockin' mustache.

SET YOUR TABLE

Be creative with your holiday parties this year and never underestimate the power of a dime store party favor.

Two of a Kind

When hearts and holiday ornaments align: last summer, Mike and I went with our movie club to the Grove Park Inn in Asheville, North Carolina. At separate times, we visited the gift shop. And at separate times, we bought the same Christmas tree ornament to surprise each other.

Why? Because many years ago, we fell in love as a young couple dating during a trip to this historic hotel which cemented its place in our hearts. A lot of life has happened since then and now always easy, but, thankfully, always together.

So now our hearts sit side by side on our Christmas tree, happy and content.

SET YOUR TABLE

Share an ornament that symbolizes your love for someone special.

Acknowledgments

I am forever grateful for my cherished circle of family, friends and insanely talented creatives featured in this book. Thank you, Bailey LeFever, for your keen editorial eye and heart. And, once again, a special thanks to Steve Codraro for making my words come to beautiful life with such gorgeous and unique designs!

We hope you enjoyed reading this title from:

www.blackrosewriting.com

Subscribe to our mailing list – *The Rosevine* – and receive **FREE** books, daily deals, and stay current with news about upcoming releases and our hottest authors.
Scan the QR code below to sign up.

Already a subscriber? Please accept a sincere thank you for being a fan of Black Rose Writing authors.

View other Black Rose Writing titles at www.blackrosewriting.com/books
and use promo code
PRINT to receive a **20% discount** when purchasing.

www.ingramcontent.com/pod-product-compliance
Lightning Source LLC
Chambersburg PA
CBHW071919070526
44583CB00016B/2050